DAYS OF APPREHENSION AND ADVENTURE

Experiences of Scottish Child Evacuees During World War II

by

Mattie Turnbull

DORRANCE
PUBLISHING CO
EST. 1920
PITTSBURGH, PENNSYLVANIA 15238

Dorrance Publishing Company, Inc.
585 Alpha Drive
Pittsburgh, PA 15238
Visit our website at www.dorrancebookstore.com

ISBN: 978-1-4809-2695-0
eISBN: 978-1-4809-2833-6

CHAPTER ONE:

1939 WAR IS ON ITS WAY:
WHAT SHOULD WE DO WITH THE CHILDREN?

I can never forget that the ultimate decision, the Yes or No which may decide the fate not only of all this generation but of the British Empire itself, rests with me ... Neville Chamberlain to Hilda Chamberlain, 2 April 1939 (Douglas 1978, p.1).

I have to tell you now that no such undertaking (German withdrawal from Poland) has been received and consequently this country is at war with Germany.
Prime Minister, Neville Chamberlain, addressing the nation, 3 September 1939.

(Courcy, **1989**)

How this book started

The curiosity that engendered this story was born of a Scottish childhood where there was often great banter around the dinner table, to which three generations contributed in the late 1940s and early 1950s. Much of the banter and more serious exchange focussed on World War II and the social outcomes of those harrowing six years. This was an era when ordinary people were not only craving great social change but demanding it. Inevitably as the debate in my home ebbed and flowed, the issue of the mass evacuation of children across the United Kingdom during World War II was raised and naturally in particular the Scottish experience. Although several around the table had reasonable recollections of this great undertaking, it appeared that no seminal account of the Scottish experience had been read.

The allegations made by some host families was also troubling - that many of the evacuees suffered deprivation, they were often covered in lice, that they had less-than-acceptable toilet habits and were inevitably bed wetters was often discussed. However, from many recollections from ordinary working class parents and children with much in common with the evacuees, this did not seem to be the case. In fact, most of the evacuees in this story were usually surprised at these assumptions. Indeed most indicated that they had decent clothes, albeit only one Sunday best outfit. The oldest girl child often was able to have piano and/or tap dancing lessons and the boys were occupied with sports, the Boys Brigade, and the Boy Scouts. Nevertheless, those unflattering images of the evacuees became the received wisdom of the time and prevailed for some time. These images are referred to throughout following the evacuees' remembering.

The pursuit of the Scottish Evacuation story persisted, raising awareness that even in Scotland, there was little easily accessible literature relative to the Scottish experiences. The later discussion of Big Nation/Small Nation theory aims to provide an explanation for the concentration on the English experience to the neglect of the Scottish story.

By chance, the decision to develop this work was determined by a discussion at a rather pleasant dinner party late in 2005 in Perth, Western Australia. One of the guests asked me whether or not I would do any further academic study, and I replied that I had always had an avid interest in the phenomenon of the World War II Evacuation. Serendipitously, it transpired that two of the guests, both of Scottish origin, were indeed evacuees themselves. The fact that since the 50th anniversary of the end of World War II, the interest in the experiences of 'ordinary people' had gained momentum (Lawson 2006, Gardiner 2005 and

Rose 2003) was discussed. Those who had been evacuees indicated that they would be delighted to tell their stories and the die was cast.

The British mass evacuation of children during World War II was the most ambitious and advance planned evacuation in recent history. In the evacuation process, 3.5 million people: British children, including children under school age, mothers, expectant mothers, teachers and people with disabilities, were involved in the voluntarily evacuation to the country from the cities. Mass expulsion is not necessarily *forced* expulsion. Indeed various exiles occurred during the 20th century, many involving children but all are attributable to the exercise of political power and all resulted in unexpected dislocation and separation from families. British evacuees held a unique place in the World War II conflict because they saw no action either in the theatre of war, in their billets or in their own home towns.

This story is concerned primarily with the evacuation of Scottish children from their homes in the cities to country areas, which were deemed to be safer during times of anticipated heavy bombing raids on Britain by the German Luftwaffe during World War Two. Approximately 400,000 people were involved in the Scottish evacuation and this work develops understandings of the evacuees' experiences of internal displacement and separation and contributes to the emerging child exile body of knowledge, currently a fertile field. The separation of the Scottish story from the overarching British one is of constant challenge inasmuch as, although a separate entity within the United Kingdom at the time, Scotland did not have the same level of autonomy as that of a province in Canada or a state in Australia.

In both size and population, Scotland is a small country (5m) relative to England/Wales/Northern Ireland (59m). Politically and socially, Scotland has differed in many ways throughout its history. These differences contributed to an alternative approach to many social undertakings, including the evacuation of thousands of children from their homes often to be cared for by strangers.

Because the United Kingdom encompasses Scotland, England, Wales and Northern Ireland, and because much of the literature alludes to the Scottish experiences only within those of England, it was difficult to isolate the Scottish Evacuation experience from the British one. The story is therefore developed from the primary research outcomes from the participants and the secondary research outcomes available from the literature and historical archives.

The main aim of this story/account is to develop understandings of the Scottish evacuees' experiences of internal displacement and separation with a view to increasing the knowledge of the Scottish Evacuation experience in all its richness and diversity. It compares the evacuees' experiences with the emerging body of knowledge of child exile experiences; it interrogates the underlying ideologies, cultural practices and understandings that enabled mass Evacuation of children to take place; and it positions the Scottish Evacuation practices and policies in Scotland within the wider practices and policies on Evacuation in the United Kingdom as a whole. The work covers several major areas of inquiry that are inextricably bound.

Although this research is confined primarily to Scotland, and the movement of children within Scotland (and within the British context), there is a large and growing interest in, and investigation of, the movements of children from Britain to the colonies during the 20th century and, more widely such displacement of children in other regions of the world (Research Centre for Evacuee and War Child Studies: University of Reading, established 2004)[1]. Many of the evacuees held the perception that their experiences were largely forgotten with regard to war and post-war history which includes the great social changes which swept post-war Britain and this was an interesting and somewhat common thread running across most of the participants' sentiments. However, the importance and relevance of the Evacuation has been acknowledged, particularly since 1997.

Understandably then, a substantial literature gives emphasis to the English/Welsh child evacuation experience. This work therefore fills the gap in the complete evacuation story by telling of the Scottish experiences which have been less well documented. The gap was filled by the exploration of the experiences of 51 evacuees, 38 originally from Scotland and 13 originally from England. Follow-up interviews were also conducted with seven of the participants. The Scottish evacuees at the time of their exile lived primarily in the West of Scotland and their socio-economic backgrounds were mainly from the working class, as was the situation of the English evacuees. The rich data which emanated from these in-depth interviews have encapsulated what it meant to have been a Scottish evacuee during World War Two.

The research shows that the approach to the process in Scotland differed considerably from the processes in England/Wales although embedded in a similar framework. It is therefore appropriate and of great importance that the Scottish story has its place in the British evacuation history. Concurrently the Scottish evacuation experiences contribute to the knowledge and understandings of this significant social phenomenon. (Much has also been written of the Northern Ireland Evacuation experience)

It is acknowledged that the participants were telling their stories through a lens of more than 60 years separation from the event. This is in itself is a social phenomenon of sorts.

Essentially the purpose of this book is to record and reflect on

> *the experiences of Scottish child evacuees and their valued contribution to the knowledge of British child evacuation during World War Two.*

To this end, the following approach was used:
- to develop understandings of the Scottish evacuees' experiences of internal exile and separation;
- to examine the reasons for the apparent neglect of the Scottish Evacuation experiences;
- to position the Scottish Evacuation within the wider Evacuation policies which were implemented in the United Kingdom and overseas as a whole;
- to contribute to the body of knowledge of child exile experiences;
- to demonstrate the importance of memory and remembrance as they relate to the evacuees experiences;
- to relate the Evacuation experience to the development and implementation of the British Welfare State; and
- to interrogate the underlying ideologies, cultural practices and understandings that enabled mass Evacuation of children to take place.

Based on the above, the Scottish evacuation story, hitherto a largely neglected event, is now told.

CHAPTER TWO:

EVACUATION: DEVELOPMENT,
PLANNING AND IMPLEMENTATION: Operation Pied Piper[2]

*I suppose that because the bombing had already started and we were
all aware of it, that my parents thought it [Evacuation] was the
obvious thing to do* (Isobel from Glasgow).

**GOVERNMENT
EVACUATION
SCHEME**

The Government have ordered evacuation
of school children.

If your children are registered for
evacuation send them to their assembly
point at once.

If your children are not registered and
you wish them to be evacuated, the
teachers or the school keeper will help you.

If you do not wish your children to
be evacuated you must not send them to
school until further notice.

Posters notifying the arrival of parties in
the country will be displayed at the schools at
which the children assembled for evacuation.

*Evacuation Notice
(Westall 1995)*

In the first part of this chapter the development and application of the British
Evacuation policies relative to World War II are discussed. The second centres
on the Scottish Evacuation experiences and demonstrates that although there

were many similarities with the overarching British Evacuation, several significant differences also existed. These differences eventuated because the Evacuation was planned by the Ministry and Department of Health of the Westminster Parliament and was initially to be implemented only in the city of London in the southeast of England (Titmuss 1950, n.d). However, as the planning evolved to include Scotland, the responsibilities became largely the province of the Scottish local authorities as opposed to the Ministry and Department of Health in England. This local approach in Scotland resulted in outcomes sometimes quite unlike those in England.

Mass evacuation is not necessarily *compulsory* evacuation. Indeed several and varied exiles occurred during the 20th century, all involving children. These include the crises of the breakup of Yugoslavia, and civil wars in Africa and the Middle East, several of which are still being played out in 2015. To define compulsory or forced is problematic but suffice to say that all Evacuations or exiles which occur in periods of conflict (as opposed to natural disasters), are attributable to the exercise of political power and all result in unexpected dislocation and separation from home and families. However, the crucial difference between the British war Evacuation and others is that it was at all times voluntary (Stewart and Welshman 2006, p.105).

The planning, the politics, and statistics of this undertaking are delineated in this chapter. The Scottish Evacuation is examined, highlighting some of the differences between the Scottish approach and those of other parts of the country. The narratives of the participants, whose stories are being told for the first time in over sixty years, illustrate and bring the Evacuation Phenomenon to life and give voice to some of the children who played a part in it. When reflecting on the complexities and anxieties of the Evacuation undertaking, it must be remembered that these were very tense times and the view was held across the country that should war ensue, there was little doubt that Britain would be invaded sooner than later.

Over time, as expected, other accounts of the Evacuation have been written and published by those who were not actually part of the event, but this research ensures that the reminiscences of the Scottish participants bear fruit as the central theme of the story. One of the major statistical and social accounts of the Evacuation is provided by Richard Titmuss, who was Professor of Social Administration at the London School of Economics from 1950 until his death in 1973. He played an important role in establishing social policy and administration as scientific disciplines both in Britain and internationally: his thinking and writing helped to shape the British Welfare State. His account of the Evacuation was commissioned by British Official Histories (*History of the Second World War*) General Series. Although Richard Titmuss is the acknowledged historian of the Evacuation, several of the stories of the participants sometimes ran counter to the accounts written by him. These are interspersed throughout this work, not only in this chapter, but progressively as the Evacuation story unfolds.

The lack of analytical rigour at the broadest level in previous works relative to the Evacuation process and undertaking is lamented by Crosby (1986) who suggests that the works written and available about the phenomenon preclude a broad understanding because of the tendency to limit the research to anecdotal claims and accounts primarily from the receiving households. These anecdotes abound, mostly deriving from the well-intentioned policy of endeavouring to bring together the various strands of British social structure during the period. Indeed, it was an aspiration of some of the country's leaders that far reaching social reform would emanate from this unintended social experiment. These leaders included, for example, Ramsay MacDonald, Prime Minister from 1931 to 1935 and John Maynard Keynes, the economist (Holman 1995, p.114).

With the benefit of hindsight, it seems unwise to have expected a social experiment of such magnitude to be unproblematic when it placed relatively poor (in an economic sense) inner city children and parents with affluent country residents or farming communities, a completely different sector of society in a highly urbanised country such as the United Kingdom. Certainly, to imagine that this mixing of relatively privileged and underprivileged people in unfamiliar and unexpected circumstances would result in harmonious relations was naïve at best. To illustrate the absurdity of the manifestation of the social cleavages existing during the Evacuation period, this interesting and troubling, but contextually amusing, exchange was made between a householder and her charge in the South of England: 'When Rita Friede, a Jewish girl, arrived in her foster home (billet) the woman began to look in her hair: I said to her, "We've got clean heads, what are you looking for?" and she said, "I'm looking for your horns'." This remark encapsulates the confusion experienced by both the evacuees and the receiving households about each other (Wicks 1988, p.95).

Crosby (1986) devotes a significant portion of his work to the importance and relevance of class in the Evacuation experience confirmed by others noted above. He suggests that the prevailing view *of* the poor (but not *by* the poor) was that they would panic when bombs started to fall in their high-density living areas. These assumptions were made by the Evacuation planners, and the civil servants, i.e. those who held public office, who were, by and large, of a middle and upper class background. However, it does appear that the level of ignorance of the better off about those less well-off was ill-informed. Naturally, many anecdotes of the poor reflect equal ignorance of the more affluent (Crosby 1986). Because of the renewed interest in the Evacuation in the past 20 years, there is no doubt that opinions beyond those of Crosby will be forthcoming. It is acknowledged that many evacuees were from a middle class background but they were often evacuated privately. Nevertheless, the vast majority of the participants in this work were from a working class background and from an inner city environment.

Prelude to Development of the Evacuation Policy

The period from 1929 to 1939 was one of great social unrest across Britain. This unrest was essentially related to the high number of unemployed as well as an increasing interest in the politics of the Left. As a counterpoint to the ideological Leftist position held by many in the country's universities as well as the unemployed, the Conservative government under the leadership of Stanley Baldwin, Prime Minister from 1935 to 1937 generated a period of strong economic recovery from the depression years, but this prosperity was largely confined to the South East of the country (Addison 1975, p.26). Nevertheless, the then Conservative government had introduced several social initiatives in the areas of health and education across the country which, although commendable, did not appear able to assuage the concerns of the people regarding the slow pace of social change. Regardless of the progress made by the conservative political position, the social divide caused by mass unemployment became a serious political issue spanning the conflicting political ideologies of the time. Britain was the scene not only of domestic unrest but also, the increasing threat of war exacerbated the complexities of loyalties, governance and party politics (Douglas 1978, pp. 7-11).

Although Adolf Hitler (the German Chancellor) had been in power in Germany since 1933, the 1935 British election was conducted in a time when the economy was recovering and war did not seem imminent. However, rumours that the government was planning to introduce compulsory military service as well as to build up British armaments were rife and these issues were to play an important role in the next few years as the build up to war intensified (Childs 1995, p.17).

By 1936, although the likelihood of war was being seriously considered there still remained on the part of all political parties a great reluctance to enter another military conflict. This general reluctance to go to war was based on several factors suggested by Hughes (2007, p.49). One was the optimism of Prime Minister Neville Chamberlain, who believed that the British rearmament and its deterrent capacity were beginning to 'impress Hitler'. Hughes explained Chamberlain's optimism was based on the suggestion that, due to Hitler's awareness of the possibility of a British build-up of a military capacity, this might deter Germany from attacking the United Kingdom. Secondly, the then Leader of the Opposition, Ramsay McDonald, had also assumed a pacifist approach to another war, a position he had held prior to World War One (Addison 1975, p.27). Despite this optimism, there were important underlying issues that could not be ignored: the aggrandisement position assumed by Hitler which the British government anticipated would inevitably render a violent outcome. Therefore, the parliament considered that a pacifist approach might neutralise a convincing challenge to its imperial position in the world by a newly-revived German self-confidence. For a time Britain believed that the maintenance of the status quo, that is, continuing dialogue between Britain and Germany in an endeavour to avoid war, should be pursued for as long as possible. This was accepted by the Parliament as the least risky approach to Adolph Hitler's imperialist designs within Europe (Childs 1995, 35).

These dilemmas put the government in a parlous and unenviable position. The fact that the British government, faced with the precariousness of impending war, encountered high levels of uncertainty from His Majesty's Opposition as well as the public, is not surprising (Hughes 2007, p.38). The conflicting attitudes by parliamentarians and public intellectuals in both Britain and France were widespread during the 1930s. These related to preparedness for war, as well as to perceptions of the military and air power of Germany. This was a major concern for many in Britain, as it was feared that Germany could deal an initial knockout blow to the South of England, the most highly populated region of the country. The government was also concerned with how to deal politically with the horrendous prospect of another world war, fewer than twenty years after the trench warfare which had resulted in the enormous casualty figures of World War One. No doubt influenced by these recent memories, as well as by a politician's desire for self-preservation, the British Prime Minister from 1937 to 1940, Neville Chamberlain, had persevered with a policy of appeasing Germany. With hindsight of course, Chamberlain's dogged pursuit of appeasement now seems naïve. However, for a time, he successfully argued that appeasement would reduce European tensions and offer an opportunity to develop treaties of non-aggression and an international understanding on limitation of arms production (Colvin 1971, 35-45).

A re-assessment of the meeting held in Munich in September 1938 of the four-power conference (France, Britain, Germany and Italy), based on Chamberlain's appeasement position, was written as recently as 2008. This reflection offers further insight about the position of Chamberlain whose ingenuousness regarding the trustworthiness of Hitler, according to Faber (2008, nap.), was obvious. Chamberlain believed that Hitler would pursue further goals by peaceful means whereas in fact, no sooner was the conference over than Hitler invaded the Sudetenland (a German speaking province of Czechoslovakia). Faber contradicts the popular perception that the Munich conference had been convened to determine if Germany could occupy the Sudeten territory but demonstrates that this had already been conceded. In fact, the conference was concerned with the timing of the occupation of the province: not whether it would happen but when it would happen.

Apart from Chamberlain's efforts to negotiate with Germany, Britain's depleted armed forces, and government consciousness of the public mood towards another war were important factors in Britain's unwillingness to engage in another conflict (Freedman 1999, p. 18; Vessey 2003 n.p.). According to Taylor (1972, p.116), a policy of appeasement was pursued also due to political support for a similar approach to that of World War One: a defensive war to resist aggression.

But future Prime Minister Winston Churchill supported a major increase in armaments production. This move was made in the face of much cynicism across the country, not least because of concerns regarding the slow pace of social reform, a direct consequence of the Depression, and the need to provide employment and adequate living conditions. There existed across the country, the widespread belief that the government should direct funding to issues other than armament manufacture. Although the Labour Opposition's official war position was the pursuit of pacifism, many members of the elected parliamentary party supported increased arms spending and preparation for war (Wicks 1988). From a quite different ideological perspective, Prime Minister Stanley Baldwin and Minister Chamberlain fought against the establishment of a centralised Ministry of Supply, continuing to argue that increased government expenditure was a 'great evil' (Taylor 1972, p.119). Throughout the 1930s, therefore, the British government endeavoured to avoid war at almost any price, for all the reasons noted above. Nevertheless, political differences aside, the parties agreed to offer a defence guarantee to Poland in August 1939. Subsequent therefore to Germany's invasion of Poland 1 September 1939, the British and French governments declared war on Germany on 3 September (Douglas 1978, p.63).

Due to the ambiguity regarding a possible war across the political spectrum, it is understandable that the development of the Evacuation policy during the 1930s suffered from as much uncertainty as did the road to war itself. The population could well understand the notion of and necessity for something called Civil Defence; but Evacuation was not yet seriously in the consciousness of the decision makers or the population; and the people's reluctance to contemplate another war no doubt resulted in the authorities' disinclination to publicise any Evacuation plans. Therefore it was not until early in 1938 that the most rudimentary plans were being studied very carefully (Titmuss 1950, n.p.).

Ambivalence

In recognizing the potential magnitude of war casualties, the government determined that a large exodus from London and other cities was inevitable and, unless the government took firm control, panic, chaos and confusion were bound to ensue. But there remained the important dimension of the process of Evacuation which was the issue of uncertainty: the authorities' undecided approach towards the welfare of the children, and the people's own mood towards the war and emerging Evacuation policies of the state. The government's ambivalence towards the welfare of the children to be evacuated can be found in the accounts by Titmuss (1950, n.p.). He suggests that Evacuation was regarded *simply and solely as a military expedient*, a counter-move to the enemy's objective of attack and demoralization of the civilian population. But as it turned out, the reality was that the social implications of a voluntary undertaking possibly unequalled in civilian history, *not* those of the military engagement, emerged as the most far-reaching. Uncertainty was also shared by parents, who, while understanding that the policy had their children's safety at heart, knew war had not yet been declared. Therefore, why should the plans for Evacuation be so entrenched when Chamberlain was still waving his white piece of paper? As Jenny (from Clydebank) remembers when asked if she felt the Evacuation was necessary, she mused:

> *Well, I haven't thought much about that, but now that you ask, perhaps many people would think it was. But I know my Mother would never have parted with me. On the other hand, it was war and I suspect lots of people would not be here today if it* [the Evacuation] *hadn't happened. We did what were told in those days and that includes my Mother. After all, it was for our own good.*

and Stewart (from Edinburgh) said:

> *I suspect they supported the process: an ill wind and all that. I'd say they would have thought it was probably good for children. By that I mean they thought it would be a good experience. But as private evacuees, we were much protected because we had options and were not dependent on anyone like other evacuees. I'm sure it would have been quite different if we had been billeted or if children were on their own without their mother.*

The notion that strange decisions have been made throughout history for the alleged good of those who were affected by them is the subject of Anna Haebich's influential work (1992) which documents and considers the events of what has become known as The Stolen Generations in Australia. During this period, many Indigenous Australian children were taken from their homes and families because it was assumed that the children's family arrangements and their living conditions were so bad that they had to be taken away. This allegedly ensured that their financial situation would be improved, they would enjoy an enhanced cultural experience, and would receive a better education. With such provision, they would have the chance to become useful members of society in the homes of Australians of European descent. But, it was claimed by those in charge of this policy, as in the British Evacuation policy, that its measures were indeed for the children's own good, the prevailing orthodoxy. Crucial to this account is acceptance of this paradox: movement of their children to safety, yet giving them up to strangers for an unknown period of time. Not only would children be separated from their families at vulnerable and susceptible ages, they were often placed with families from vastly different social and economic backgrounds (Rose 2003, p.57).

Planning for Evacuation

Mass Evacuation was an integral component of the overall Civil Defence planning prior to the advent of war (declared September 3, 1939) and initially the British Ministry of Health based in London took responsibility for facilitating the undertaking. But in due course in Scotland this became the task of the local authorities in consultation with the Scottish Department of Health.

Although the idea of an imminent war was not necessarily in the consciousness of the leaders at that time, a potential future conflict in Europe was recognised. Therefore with the acknowledgement of the possibility that a considerable number of tons of bombs per day could be dropped in Britain with resultant human casualties, the Evacuation plans in the event of major conflagration began to take shape (Brown, 2000, p.2). Some intermittent contemplation of an Evacuation plan had been conveyed to the Committee of Imperial Defence between 1924 and 1929, and by 1933 the idea of Evacuation had been subsumed into the integrated system of civil defence which had already been authorised. But by 1934, this scheme was expanded to include the whole of the country (United Kingdom) and the plan was officially agreed (Brown 2000, p.2). The Evacuation debates were conducted against a background of national and European political concerns which were to become critical during the prelude to the war (Wicks 1988, p.12). By May 1938, as the likelihood of another war loomed, the government established a sub-committee of the Department of Civil Defence (the Anderson Committee) dedicated to the development of an Evacuation policy (Brown 2000, p.3).

During the committee's initial deliberations, the order of population categories to be evacuated became an issue of contestation: the Anderson Committee originally suggested that all but essential workers should be first to be evacuated from London, but the London County Council was of the view that mothers and children, accompanied by their teachers, should be first. This order was based on the argument that to move the children would be a more complex operation than the movement of adults. According to Holman (1995, pp.10-12), there was great confusion regarding the responsibility for overseeing the Evacuation: who should be in charge and how would the evacuees be prioritised? The Evacuation policy was also born of the proposition that during another war, morale would be a significant factor. However in the event, school children and mothers with children of pre-school age were given first priority in transport and billeting facilities. The anticipated level of incendiary bombing was primarily the stimulus for the development of the Evacuation policy as the government observed that the quickening pace of German rearmament had overtaken that of the Royal Air Force. But in fact, the roots of any future Evacuation had grown from the bombardment of London by German Zeppelins and planes during World War One. In this bombardment, 1,117 civilians were killed (Colvin 1971, p.23). Of particular apprehension to the British was the accelerated expansion of the German manufacture of weapons of war, including sophisticated air power, after World War One and in particular from 1931. Although Britain had been secure from invasion for almost a thousand years, the possibility of German bombs reaching the British mainland was a realistic potential outcome which could result in a level of destruction hitherto thought incomprehensible (Brown 2000, p.2).

The first attempt to translate the principle of Evacuation into detailed plans was an initial comprehensive report developed by the Anderson Committee (headed by Sir John Anderson, MP)[3], completed in July 1938 and immediately submitted to the Home Secretary. Railway and other transport timetables were developed, which was a lengthy and complicated process, with an estimated cost to the government in the region of £920,000 a week. It proposed that control should be exercised by the police, that Evacuation should be voluntary, that complete families should wherever possible move together, and that these persons should be accommodated in billets within fifty miles from London. The Evacuation was initially to be out of London only.

In October 1938, the planning was given legitimacy to proceed, with overall responsibility being given to Sir John Anderson, now promoted to the role of Lord Privy Seal. He took charge of all civil defence planning which included the Evacuation, but only in late July 1939, were the Evacuation's operational responsibilities formalised (Crosby 1986, p.9). One of the first tasks of the planning process was to draw new boundary lines throughout Britain, dividing the country into three zones: Evacuation, Neutral and Reception. This was accomplished by January 1939. The classifications by the Ministry of Health and its departments were defined - see undernoted - and assisted by advice from the Ministry of Defence acknowledging the necessity that somehow accommodation had to be found for 3,500,000 persons in England /Wales, and a further 400,000 in Scotland. Relative to the Scottish Evacuation, indications were that the undertaking was being planned with only limited formal support from the Department of Health for Scotland based in Edinburgh, in due course relying largely on the local authorities in the receiving areas (Titmuss 1950, n.p.; Holman 1995, p.10; Boyd 1944, p.8).

Initially, over two hundred local authorities in England and Wales, graded as Reception, asked to be re-ranked as Neutral (neither to send nor receive evacuees), and a further sixty authorities requested that they be scheduled for Evacuation. This situation resulted in great conflict and was ultimately resolved by the Department of Civil Defence, a Division in the Home Office, in consultation with the Department of Health (Westminster). The various protagonists resolved that if the concessions requested were agreed to, this would logically result in a large number of sending, but limited numbers of receiving areas, and the problem of accommodation would become insoluble. Therefore most of these representations for a change in status or zone were rejected (Holman 1995, p.10). It is reflective of the temper of the country at the time that no authority zoned as Evacuable disputed the Ministry of Health's decision, but concomitantly no authority asked to be a Reception area. Clearly Evacuation was viewed as less onerous than Reception (Titmuss 1950, n.p.).

Given the remoteness of some rural areas, far away from railway and major road routes, the anticipated safe removal of around four million people was a mammoth undertaking. Nonetheless, in the first stage of the Evacuation, between June and September 1939, two million private evacuees across mainland Britain, were safely removed from the cities to be accommodated in the country. Subsequently, the official/government Evacuation began on the first of September when approximately three million government evacuees were removed to the country over a three day period (Holman 1995, p.12). The private evacuees were accommodated by family and friends in rural Britain, but the private accommodation was not included in the government accommodation census and no billeting allowance was made for those who offered accommodation on a private basis. Initially, all householders were advised to make private arrangements for their own safety which, as suggested by Brown (2000, p.13), was an indicator that the planners anticipated or presumed a reality quite out of touch with the lives of many of the urban working class: how many working class or indeed middle class families would have had access to private accommodation in the rural and regional areas of the country?

The official Evacuation would involve large numbers of people descending on small townships, sometimes without adequate warning or preparation and would require the utilisation of vast resources in order to ensure appropriate provisions. The Evacuation Committee published its final report on 27 October 1938. The report outlined the immense logistical problems related to the potential movement of hundreds of thousands of people into perhaps not fully prepared country reception areas and cautioned that more preparation would need to be undertaken and immediately. The poor planning and anticipation of the seriousness of the situation gave the then Opposition political parties an opportunity to accuse the government of dereliction of duty with regard to civil defence. Fortunately the immediate threat of heavy bombing passed during the few months from September 1939 to April 1940, giving an opportunity to plan the Evacuation more strategically (Holman 1995, p.29).

In order to ensure the uptake of the Evacuation process, many public sector authorities also had to show or demonstrate their support of the policy to the citizens. This support was promoted by agencies such as schools, local councils, (both those who administered the transport processes and those who received the evacuees and administered the billeting), health departments and public transport authorities. Volunteer groups such as the Women's Voluntary Services and the Women's Institute were also at the cutting edge of the operation, working closely with government departments and local authorities, initially with the Evacuation process but later in many war conflict support roles (*WVS War History n.d*).

The initial response to the official Evacuation process was wide-ranging but with huge disparities across regions. For example, the number of those willing to join the undertaking in Scotland was higher than in outer London. As noted above, Titmuss (1950, n.p.) suggests that the higher response rates in Scotland were the result of a low socio-economic demographic. This suggests that poorer families were more easily convinced that Evacuation would be a wise undertaking for their children's safety on the basis that their betters knew best. Overall, the official reports (Titmuss 1950, n.p.) suggest that the Evacuation policy was met with more support than rejection and the issues which assisted the acceptance of the Evacuation policy included the notion of National Identity constructed and defined through film, posters, songs and subliminal representations such as the media's reporting of the danger of invasion. These became integral to the notion of national belonging together with the virtues of self-sacrifice, relentless cheerfulness stoicism and obligation (Rose 2003). This construction, it is argued, facilitated acceptance of the extraordinary concept of mass Evacuation and is considered more fully through the narratives of the participants more fully later.

As noted above, subsequent to the commencement of war, the Evacuation policy was quickly implemented with the support of those who were to be exiled from the cities to often unknown parts of the country. The question of public morale was crucial to the designers of the social policy. Those in the most vulnerable parts of the country would need to leave their homes, family, and security as soon as possible. Since, according to the planners of the time, women and children could not be expected to behave in the same disciplined and ordered way as the armed forces, the possibility of panic became a major concern in the delivery of the Evacuation process: but there also existed the threat that the organisers and those involved, the children, the parents, the teachers and those who billeted the evacuees, would themselves contribute to the potential for disorder (Macnicol 1986, p.24; Titmuss 1950, n.p.). Developing a strategy to deal with the horrendous prospect of another world war, fewer than twenty years after the huge casualty figures of the World War One, became paramount to British political and social policy, which included the Evacuation. Although the Evacuation resulted in unhappiness for many of those evacuated, the sheer numbers who were successfully relocated has been acknowledged as a mark of the policy's success (Parsons 1998, p.7).

However, the compulsory mixing of classes of the Evacuation in a heavily class-based society not surprisingly, had not the most successful of outcomes. Within Scotland, mothers took their children home in large numbers during the first few months of the war: by the end of October 1939, an estimated 75 per cent of those from the Receiving Areas had returned (Boyd 1944, p.31). It is possible that the high number of those who returned was due to the Phoney War the period from September 1939 - April 1940, during which, the expected *blitzkrieg* by Germany did not eventuate (Grafton, n.p). However, although a high proportion of evacuees did go home after short stays in their billets during the Phoney War, other exoduses occurred in 1940 (and in 1941 in Scotland) as a result of German air attacks, and again in 1944 as V-2 rockets were dropped on London and the South East of England. The response to the blitz on Glasgow and Clydebank is dealt with later in this chapter.

Although it had been expected that up to 3.5 million people would be evacuated across the country, ultimately in 1939, 827,000 schoolchildren; 524,000 mothers and children under school age; 13,000 expectant mothers; 103,000 teachers and 7,000 handicapped people were evacuated from their homes across the United Kingdom (Foster *et al.* 2003, p.399). 400,000 was the projected number of evacuees to be involved in the Evacuation in Scotland (Titmuss 1950, n.p.). The areas from which people were evacuated were deemed to be those most vulnerable to German bombing and in Scotland these areas were Glasgow, Edinburgh, Dundee, Clydebank and Rosyth.

Map of Scotland highlighting areas in Blue to which the Scottish children were evacuated (www.scotland.com/images/map-new.gif)

The areas in England included Greater London, the Medway ports, Birmingham, Coventry, Derby and Nottingham, Merseyside: Liverpool, Bootle, Wallasey, Birkenhead, Manchester and Salford, Bradford, Leeds, Sheffield, Grimsby and Middlesbrough in Yorkshire and Newcastle, Gateshead, South Shields, Jarrow on the north-east coast (Foster *et al.* 2003, p.400). Many children were also privately evacuated to other parts of the British Empire including Australia, New Zealand, Canada, South Africa, and to the United States of America. A background to this Evacuation and some of the issues surrounding these exiles are dealt with in Chapter Four.

It is interesting that the available body of literature provides only a limited account of the evacuated teachers' roles and involvement in the Evacuation, which Cunningham and Gardner (1999, pp.327-337) claim numerically to be in the region of 90,000 in England and Wales and 16,000 in Scotland. The

Scottish teachers' role during this extraordinary time was crucial not only relative to children's educational needs, but their pastoral contribution was considerable, assisting many mothers to adjust to new circumstances (Boyd 1944, p.28). Although the role of the teachers is not the focus of this research, their commitment to the welfare of the children has been recorded in some of the literature and in the participants' stories. In Scotland many mothers of the Scottish evacuees were billeted with their children, and the children recalled their teachers' positive influence. This influence was manifested in taking on the responsibility of the health and wellbeing of the children (unaccompanied minors), duties far beyond the remit of their normal teaching duties.

The Scottish Evacuation: a Different Experience

Scotland is a small country, relative to England/ Wales and the understandings of the participants indicated that the Evacuation in Scotland differed from processes in England/Wales, and although 400,000 were evacuated, only a small number of narratives of the Scottish Evacuation experience has been officially recorded (Banks n.d.) and (Boyd 1944). However, it is also evident from these writers' accounts that significant differences existed in the approach to and experiences of the Scottish children relative to the experiences of the rest of the United Kingdom. Perhaps the most significant difference was that many Scottish children (of a certain age) were accompanied with their mothers rather than by school teachers (Gardiner 2005, p.14), (Titmuss 1950, n.p.).

Although the Evacuation was a positive and exciting experience for many of the Scottish children, some of the participants were perplexed and a bit unsure about how they felt both at the time of the Evacuation and during the interviews, which were conducted at a much later stage in their lives in 2009. For example George (from Glasgow) reflected:

> *I suppose I am wondering what would happen today. I wouldn't think I would want to stay with strangers. But of course my mother was with us. Anyway if I had to be away from my mother, I think I would have just said I would stay at home with all the risks.*

The Clydebank Blitz

Although there had been a great trek back from the Evacuation billets, this was halted by a major event in the history of Scotland's war that occurred in

Clydebank in the West of Scotland, home to many of the great shipyards of the era. On the nights of the 13 and 14 March 1941, the Luftwaffe executed a brutal attack, dealing a devastating blow to the city. Of a population of 50,000, 528 people were killed. Comparison with the raids on Coventry on 14/15 November 1940 when out of a population of 200,000, 550 people were killed, reveals the gravity of the Clydebank blitz (MacPhail 1974, p.25). This resulted in a second wave of Evacuation. The extent of the carnage in Clydebank, relative to other centres, rarely achieves coverage outside of Scotland in accounts of the British war. This is surprising given the extent of the damage and loss of life. It has not attained the national significance accorded other bombed sites, such as Coventry and London. Doug (from Clydebank) recalled:

> *We lived quite close to the town centre (Clydebank). On the night of the Clydebank Blitz we heard the sirens about nine in the evening. Foolishly, we thought the sirens were from London! The difference in the bombing experience of course was that in Clydebank there was no warning – the bombs were dropping long before the sirens were sounded. There were at least 250 planes! On 13th March 1941 bombs were dropped every 15 minutes from 9.00 pm until 6.20 am.*

It is significant that no advice was given to the people of Clydebank of the possibility of attack from the air, despite the city being one of the major shipbuilding regions in mainland Britain (MacPhail 1974).

Although in the planning stages there was an apparent enthusiasm for the Evacuation plan, indications are that a low number of potential evacuees from several Scottish cities took up the options. In Edinburgh only 27 per cent of anticipated evacuees in fact left the city (*Glasgow Herald*, September 2, 1939). There were several reasons for the low uptake including concerns regarding financial precariousness, and misunderstanding the conditions of billeting. But many parents simply could not part from their children at the last minute (*The Glasgow Herald*, September 24, 1939). This lack of response to the official Evacuation process ensured that receiving areas were able to cope better than anticipated.

In common with the general anecdotal evidence of those who billeted evacuees, there existed an unreasonable expectation of the conditions of billeting by parents billeted with their children and rivalry for affection of billeted children by parents and host families. These issues caused anxiety to all involved. Financial worry from both the mothers/parents of the evacuees and those who billeted them also gave cause for concern (*The Glasgow Herald*, September 23, 1939). Nevertheless in late September 1939, the Regional Commissioner, Scottish Civil Defence Region, reported that 'the first day's efforts [23 September] in one of the greatest social experiments ever made had been carried throughout almost the whole of Scotland without a hitch' (*The Glasgow Herald*, September 24, 1939), albeit with, and perhaps due to, largely reduced numbers. Naturally, at this time, no parents or children were given the opportunity to offer their opinion on whether or not it had gone without a hitch. The Evacuation did receive some coverage in the newspapers, but news of the war eclipsed this momentous event. Nevertheless, by November *the Glasgow Herald* (November 24, 1939) noted not the numbers of those billeted, rather that 95,852 evacuees had gone home - this being the majority of those who had left in the first Evacuation exodus. Such was the enormity of the undertaking, it was perhaps inevitable that some inappropriate decisions were made and implemented by the local authorities in Scotland who were given charge of the undertaking. These decisions resulted in children often being settled idiosyncratically in areas, for example, not far from their homes. In Scotland, children from Clydebank were being billeted in Dumbarton, only a few miles away where they would have therefore been no less vulnerable than had they stayed at home (Gardiner 2005, p.11).

Approach and strategy: Scotland and England

The official report of the Anderson Committee[4] noted that the housing standard used for England and Wales was one person per habitable room, but in Scotland, where the housing shortage was serious, a lower standard was adopted of one person per room over the age of fourteen and two in the case of children under fourteen (Titmuss 1950, n.p.). Even with the use of a lower standard of houseroom per person, the Department of Health for Scotland found itself with a very small margin of accommodation. Nearly 21 percent of all the available rooms in Scotland had been privately allocated by February 1939 as against a proportion of eighteen percent in England and Wales. According to Titmuss (1950, n.p.) this higher figure was probably due to the number of English people arranging temporary accommodation in Scotland as private evacuees. The Scottish housing shortage in 1939 was exacerbated by this movement, which was due in part to the fact that historically much of the wealth of the United Kingdom has been concentrated in London and the South East of England (Modlock 2006, n.p.). This level of wealth enabled many families to organise private Evacuations, often to Scotland which in turn reduced the number of available government billets. Because private accommodation was organised prior to the official process, this resulted in a reduced number of billets for Scottish evacuees within Scotland and a corresponding reduction in the numbers of official English evacuees (Titmuss 1950).

Rates for billeting also varied between the two countries. Parsons (1998, p.134) suggests that the rates were set in both countries in accordance with the existing Poor Law rates (England and Wales: Provisions under Def Regs 22(5), 31(A), 32(6), Section 56 (see Table 1(b) below). In Scotland the applicable law was the *Poor Law Emergency Provision Continuance (Scotland) Act* 1925 (see Table 1(a)). It has been very difficult to establish a firm rationale for the disparate rates, but by and large the rates in Scotland and England and Wales were:

Scotland 1942:

Age	Rate of Board
5 years and under 10 years	10s 6d per week per child
10 years and under 12 years	11s per week per child
12 years and under 14 years	12s per week per child
14 years and under 16 years	13s per week per child
16 years and under 17 years	15s 6d per week per child
17 years and over	16s 6d per week per person

England and Wales 1942:

Age	Rate of Board
Individual child	10s 6d per child per week
More than one child in same billet	8s 6d per child per week
Child under school age with mother	5s per week per adult
(lodging only)	3s per week per child
Teachers, helpers (lodging only)	5s per week

Both sets of rates were re-negotiated over time as deemed appropriate (Boyd 1944, p. 25).

Another difference between the Scottish and the English policy and administration are as noted earlier: in England/Wales the Ministry of Health was charged with the responsibility for control and administration of the Evacuation and reception; whereas in Scotland the responsibility for reception of evacuees was to a large extent delegated by the Scottish Department for Health and the Secretary of State for Scotland, to the local authorities.

The Departmental correspondence reveals that fundamental, if idiosyncratic, differences in approaches to the undertaking existed. For example, the government in London often broadcast by radio contradictory statements on the assumption that conditions across Britain were the same. These included using terminology such as 'town hall' which has limited application in Scotland; that only 24 hours' notice was given in Scotland of the implementation of the Evacuation, and that an 'English' broadcast was issued separately which caused confusion. One circular relative to Scotland read that 'children under school age can be taken only if mother or some other responsible person can go with them and if there were school children in the family, the family must stay together'. This is quite different from the circular relative to England which stated 'parents are urged to let their children go'. Finally, a Scottish Office report (Scotland Office n.p.) states 'we do not want to urge parents strongly to let their children go because we are short of room in the receiving areas ... we have had to include the Glasgow and Edinburgh suburban districts in the sending areas'. The examples indicate significant differences in the policies determining the Scottish and English evacuation strategies. The strategies might reasonably have created some misunderstanding.

As opposed to the process in England, schoolchildren in Scotland and those of preschool age, did not always travel in school parties but were evacuated with their mothers albeit by the same transport mode. When Scottish mothers chose to be evacuated with their children (not only pre-school), this meant that many fathers, if not in military service, remained at home due to their 'essential worker' status (Boyd 1944, p.121). As Alec from Glasgow recalls:

> *Dad seemed to think it was acceptable* [for us to go without Mum] *but Mum really didn't get over 'letting her boys go' even if it was for their own good. Dad let Mum get on with those kinds of arrangements. I mean women organised the children and the home*

in those days. I often thought about that over the years because my father was not one for the kitchen - at least not that I ever saw. But he was a good man and a good worker.

Both John and his brother Alec (from Glasgow) reflected on their own experiences (who were aged eight and eleven at the time of their Evacuation):

We were never too sure why our Mum didn't come with us [to the north of Scotland from Glasgow] *but we think now that she probably felt she should stay to look after Dad. We think she was torn between us and Dad and interpreted 'doing her duty' as looking after him. It was unlike her to make a decision like that. Anyway we didn't ask her. But the teachers were great – like a second Mum as we say. Some of them were quite young and would probably not have had children of their own.*

Matthew (from Glasgow) who was sent to Auchterarder, Perthshire, responded:

In answer to your question [Have you ever discussed the Evacuation before?], *the answer is 'no'. This is not because I don't think it was important because it was and I have read bits and pieces over the years. It's because no-one ever asked me. For me although I was a bit nervous when we were leaving to go on the train to Auchterarder, mainly because hardly any of my pals went away, it turned out to be a bit of a holiday or adventure. The people were nice at the house we stayed in although they were rich by comparison with us and that made us a bit nervous too. It's been good recollecting it all though. Perthshire is a lovely county isn't it? Let me know immediately your book gets out there.*

Kenneth (from Glasgow who went to Ardrossan), Ayrshire:

You know, it's all coming back to me because of our session today. I haven't thought about it in years so bear with me. Yes, my mother, me, my little brother and my sister (aged 10, 8 and 5) went on the train to Ardrossan. I've been there so many times in my life usually on my way somewhere else and do you know, I hardly even think about it or look at the place we stayed. I don't think the place we stayed was very clean somehow because for a couple of years after we went home Mum used to lament that her own home was much nicer than the one we got evacuated to. Because it was minutes to the sea, we enjoyed that part of it but we were confined in the tenement flat we stayed in. There was only one child in the place and she was much older than us so we didn't have much to do with her. The whole thing was a bit of a non-event actually but nothing bad happened to us.

Although many estimates can be found of the numbers of people evacuated, it could be argued that the following sources are those with most legitimacy and cogency since they were compiled by government bodies. Ultimately the number of people evacuated in England/ Wales was 1,754,970 and in Scotland, 175,066 (Titmuss 1950, n.p.). In 1939, the population of England/Wales was 39,545,332 (UK National Statistics Hub) and in Scotland it was 5,000,000 (General Register for Scotland). It is important to note that these figures compute to the exodus of Scottish children being 3.5 percent of its population and the English and Welsh exodus was 4.4 percent of their joint population. Thus proportionately the number of Scottish children evacuated was only slightly lower than the combined exodus from England and Wales. Given these numbers, the Scottish Evacuation is indeed a largely neglected event.

That it appears to have taken more than 60 years for many of the Scottish stories to be formally or academically acknowledged is extraordinary given that there are so many accounts of the English Evacuation including contemporary and recent studies: (Owen 1940; Westall 1995; Palmer 1997; Gardner 2005; Rose 2003;). The apparent lack of interest for six decades is quite remarkable given the magnitude of the event and the perpetual and avid interest in World War Two by the entertainment world, the plethora of history books, the participants' consciousness, and ongoing fascination for World War Two in general.

The importance of Boyd

Although rather limiting due to its focus on education, there is one valuable scholarly source related to Scotland's Evacuation, *Evacuation in Scotland 1944*, written by William Boyd, Reader in Education at Glasgow University and supported by the Scottish Council for Research in Education. In more recent works, Devine and Finlay 1996, and Stewart and Welshman 2006, have also utilised Boyd's seminal work.

Boyd's work on the Scottish experience is a chronicle of the more significant educational outcomes following the Evacuation story from the time of the official inception through the months of the initial undertaking and beyond. Although Boyd's focus was primarily education and thus not directly related to this topic, his statistical data in particular have been of significance for analysis. Importantly, it should be noted that Boyd's account was written in 1944, one year before the end of hostilities, which means that his research was inconclusive relative to the effects and outcomes of the experiences of those involved, since some evacuees did not return to their homes until 1945 or later. Boyd's work interestingly includes the fact that the Clydebank evacuees were categorized in accordance with whether they were of Catholic or Protestant religious persuasion. Their billeting arrangements were based on this sectarian divide. Although there is some anecdotal evidence that the children's religion did sometimes impact on successful billeting, this was not a feature of formal placement of the Scottish evacuees from areas other than Clydebank. I suggest this was due in some part to the large influx of Irish labour which was drawn to the industrial West of Scotland during the 19th and early 20th centuries and which is a focus of the work of Lynch (1996).

Boyd's research centres on three significant elements: the historical, which encompasses the period from the notional and the planning to the migration and its decline; the studies carried out by the Education Department of Glasgow University through questionnaires; and the study of a representative sample of the whole school population in a Scottish burgh. This research took the form of meetings within which parents were interviewed by their children's teachers. Boyd's account is given in meticulous administrative detail which is of great value. Sending areas and receiving areas are outlined; timelines are noted; numbers of registrants, response rates, responsibilities, costs, drift-back statistics, type of accommodation, social structures, and the selection process are all discussed and analysed. But the limitation (for purposes of this thesis) of this otherwise invaluable account of the Scottish experience is that it does not investigate distinctions between the Scottish and other Evacuations. Further, as noted above, the report was written before the end of the war thus precluding narrative or depiction of the social consequences of the experiment or experience after the war or of the evacuees' homecomings. Nevertheless, this statistical information was of great interest to the participants who, by and large, had no idea of the magnitude of the Evacuation undertaking.

A limited survey (under the direction of Boyd and included in his 1944 work) was undertaken in Clydebank one year after the Blitz (1942) under the auspices of Glasgow University which related to three questions:

- the children who were not evacuated - why and what did they do if their schools were closed?
- the children who returned - why?
- the children who did not return - why?

The results indicate that children who were not evacuated were not inclined when indications were that schools would be re-opened. Many of those who did not return were often billeted with friends and family (private Evacuations). But those who did return did so:

- because of the billets' proximity to their own homes (home posed no greater threat);
- the inability of parents to pay a proportion of their stay;
- illness of householder;
- illness of a child;
- changes in the billeter's arrangements;
- parents thought child was not cared for properly;
- child too far away for visits by parent;
- Religious difficulties (Boyd 1944, pp.114-115).

It should be borne in mind that Boyd's statistics refer only to the government scheme evacuees.

Given such an enormous undertaking, the memories and narratives of the children varied from 'a great adventure' to 'if you were a child with glasses or spots, you were always left till the end' [by receiving families] (Wicks 1988, p.59). As Betty (from Clydebank) recalled:

By the way, while we were in Dunoon, the port of Greenock was bombed which was where we had gone in the taxi to escape to in the first place (from Clydebank).

Douglas (a very tall Londoner):

I was last to be picked and I presume now that it was because I was a big lad: much taller than the others around me and they might have thought I would eat too much.

Residential Schools/Camp Schools/Residential Clinics
Since Boyd's work was primarily related to education, he devoted three chapters to the educational strategies developed during the Evacuation period (1944, pp.137-201). Firstly, large houses were utilized as residential schools, which were established to overcome problems such as the provision of full secondary education for evacuated pupils as well as the lack of transport in more remote areas, which would prevent the children's access to education. Several of these residential schools were operated under the auspices of the government Evacuation scheme but were overseen by the Glasgow Education Authorities. These included Cargen House in Dumfries and the Ernespie House in Galloway both near the Scottish/English border. In all of Boyd's accounts of the residential schools attrition rates, the drift back to Glasgow was considerable. Boyd posited that this was due to the fact that they were unused to being away from home and private billeting. The absence of one of their parents added to the reasons for the children's return home.

Two Camp Schools were also established in the South of Scotland - one at West Linton and the other at Gorebridge. These venues had already had a pre-war life as camps which accommodated children who would otherwise be unable to experience life away from the cities. However these were now taken over as residential accommodation for primary age children due to the shortage of private billeting in Scotland. In England, these camp schools were designed to billet senior central or secondary school students.

Still within the purview of the Glasgow Education Authorities, several residential clinics were established which were dedicated to the care of evacuees who were deemed to be in need of some behavioural stability and the principles of the clinics were espoused as follows:

- security, affection, and discipline are fundamental needs of childhood and must be provided;
- self-confidence and stability are dependent on achievement therefore normal schooling should be aided by intensive and specialized tuition, especially in case of backwardness;
- the understanding that comes from intimate and accurate knowledge is needed for the adjustment of the unstable child (Boyd 1944, pp. 137-201).

This approach to wartime education of Scottish children confirmed the claim by Stewart and Welshman (2006, p.104) that:

> In contrast to England, the 'problem family' concept was absent from the debate and that the evidence of the health of the Scottish evacuees was impressionistic and contradictory ... and that there was an emphasis on structural rather than behavioural causes of poverty and deprivation.

They further note that the above emphasis remains a plank of Scottish Welfare principles manifested in the major policy areas of the Scottish Parliament.

Social Construction of the Evacuee
The twin concepts of the potential war and the Evacuation were exploited by the British government at the same time as the print media's reflection of the build up to war: the emotive and harrowing accounts of events in Europe. As the Evacuation policy moved towards fruition, the government capitalized on the symbolism of war utilized by the media by developing poster campaigns, which aligned with the newspapers' and newsreels' powerful images. This campaign, directed often at mothers, included posters bearing messages such as *'Mothers Send them out of London'* (Brown 2000, p.8) and *'Don't do it, Mother, leave the children where they are'* (Brown 2000, p.35). This latter poster portrayed a mother sitting beneath a tall tree wistfully considering bringing her children back from their billets. In the background is a shadowy figure of Hitler urging her to bring them back, suggesting that they would be endangered by this move. Such symbolism conceptualized and propounded the notion of parental guilt. The clear message was that to bring their children home was to expose them to severe danger. Slogans such as 'Caring for evacuees is

a National Service' and a cute poster of two small children, well dressed and smiling depicted on a postcard which reads: 'Lots of love to Mum and Dad, don't worry, this is how we're feeling' abounded. Such exhortations were deemed necessary in order to encourage more people to host the evacuees (Gardiner 2005, p.29).

Initially, the power of the images of the evacuees, with their shiny faces, clutching their favorite toys, accompanied by mums/teachers/volunteers clambering onto trains from the dangerous cities to be received by willing and caring country people, was instrumental in selling the government's Evacuation policy. These images are captured in the 1940 movie *Westward Ho!*[5] If the government was to be able to justify the exodus of approximately one million children, a level of propaganda had to be developed. By those means, the government could promote the undertaking and persuade those involved that the policy was sound. With the assistance primarily of the print media, the government was able to successfully persuade many parents and guardians to participate in the Evacuation process by constructing the happy evacuee, excited at the prospect of adventure and new experiences.

Over time, however, the media, having initially constructed the happy child evacuees, proceeded to re-construct them. From the initial depiction of shiny-faced, smiling children with their labels around their necks and their little suitcases, they became urchins, misfits, and bed-wetters who were also dirty and verminous (Adam 1975, p.138). Britain during this wartime period was a nation of significant class difference which influenced the prevailing pejorative images of the poorer classes. Soon, with the help of various state agencies, information and statistics regarding referrals from those who billeted the children, were the province of the popular press: 48 percent of the referrals concerned bedwetting; 16 percent stealing and eight percent quarrelsome behaviour. These damaging images ensured the *re*-construction of the evacuee child as rather undesirable and obviously from the lower strata of a class-ridden society (Holman 1995, p.121).

Examples from newspapers of the time include *the Scotsman's* claim that 'the real problem was … as well as the lesson of ensuring personal cleanliness and freedom from contagious disease has been learnt by experience' (1939, p.6) and *the Glasgow Herald* noted that 'the Evacuation of Glasgow children to Dumfriesshire had led to problems, with the local Education Committee claiming that a third of the children had to be excluded from school because of the presence of head lice or disease (1939, 21 Sept, p.8). *The Perthshire Advertiser* also asserted that 'from nearly all parts of the county complaints have been received concerning the verminous and filthy condition of the children … many of whom were, moreover, found to be suffering from infectious diseases such as diphtheria, impetigo, scabies and scarlet fever' (1939, 20 Sept, p.16). The media's image of the evacuee had undergone a complete transformation.

Repositioning of the Evacuees

Although some evacuees exhibited maladaptive behaviours, unfortunately sometimes interpreted as misbehaviours, Simmons (2006, p.56) points out in her research that the child evacuees have now emerged as valuable sources of information to social historians. This is largely attributed to the contemporary research undertaken by the Centre for War Child Studies at Reading University, which gives those involved the opportunity to reject the passivity and silence about their experiences which was hitherto the situation. That is not to say that any evacuee was obligated to share their memories subsequent to the war, but obviously some did, as in the case of Joan from Lambeth in London, who was evacuated when she was four years old. As Joan, a participant whom I interviewed in Adelaide, Australia, who was a member of an Evacuee Group established there in 2005, sadly recalled:

> *I wet the bed the first night and from then on I was called 'the Wet Bed Evacuee' and the woman of the house used to put a broom outside the door which signified I had wet the bed again and then she would hit me with it. I was so unhappy and at school because I was short-sighted the teacher thought I was stupid and so I was often humiliated, but I was so troubled I didn't bother to tell the teacher about my condition. I was moved around a bit to several billets but the bed-wetting continued.*

> *I was then moved to Kettering to a hostel called 'Elmbank' and my sisters joined us. We travelled by bus. It was run by the local authority and if anything, it was even worse than my experiences with the private billets. In this place, the bed wetters in the morning were made to put their knickers on their heads and they had to stand there naked and so evacuees became I suppose we would call it today outsiders.*

Although none of the Scottish participants recalled such trauma, replication of Joan's story can be found in many other publications of the Evacuation experiences. The accounts of neglect in the English experience emanate from those I interviewed and also those researched by Holman (1995), Parsons (1998); Brown (2000); and Rose (2003). This, of course, does not mean that all Scottish experiences were positive, but the unhappy elements of the Scottish participants in this study were usually of confusion regarding the Evacuation rather than ill-treatment, as Cathie (from Clydebank) recalled:

> *In a way my Evacuation experience was serendipitous because our house ended up being demolished in the Clydebank Blitz so we would not have had anywhere to live had my Mum decided to stay. My Father was already away fighting. I always think it's an ill wind that blows nobody any good, and don't forget we stayed with the nicest people when we were away. However, I think it was all a bit strange to move all those people with no real consultation if you know what I mean.*

It has been difficult to ascertain the reasons for the length of time the Scottish child evacuees' stories have taken to emerge and why they have a lower profile. This has rendered them less able or inclined to politicise their experiences as effectively as other marginalised and aggrieved groups, such as the Stolen Generations in Australia (Briskman 2003) and the Fairbridge children (Hill 2007) who have recently found their political voice. However, in common with the English experiences, the Scottish *government* evacuees came disproportionately from the poorer strata of urban society, since they lived in the more industrial sections of the cities and because the more financially secure had access to private evacuee arrangements (Boyd 1944, p.77). Due therefore to the different social backgrounds of the evacuees and their hosts, a degree of social mismatch was inevitable. Only relatively recently has the magnitude of the Evacuation process and outcomes become the subject of academic and social inquiry and that, by and large, is within the province of the English experience. The questions therefore arise why has such a monumental social undertaking has been neglected for so long and indeed, why did the evacuees themselves not feel the need to tell their stories until so long after the event?

Conclusion

This chapter has outlined the background to and the planning of the British mass Evacuation of children (and accompanying adults) during World War Two within the United Kingdom.

At this juncture, it is timely to reiterate and acknowledge that what differentiates the British World War II Mass Evacuation of children from other exoduses is that it was planned, it was voluntary, and it involved over three million people (which included organisers), rendering it arguably the most ambitious and advance planned Evacuation in history. In the Evacuation process, British children, including children under school age (five), mothers, expectant mothers, teachers and people with disabilities were voluntarily moved to the country from the cities. The aim of this vast undertaking was to protect its subjects from the anticipated German heavy bombing raids (Parsons 1998; Brown 2000).

The Evacuation process in Scotland was similar in many ways to the Evacuation process in Britain as a whole but several significant differences in the Scottish management of the Evacuation have been discussed in the chapter. These differences have been positioned within the wider practices and policies on Evacuation in Great Britain as a whole. However, the difficulty I have encountered in locating demographics, figures and narratives relative to the Scottish experience, demonstrates the core hypothesis that the Scottish Evacuation is a largely neglected event. The dearth of information suggests that the Scottish experience was of limited interest and focus to the official records and history, compared with that of the English undertaking. To address this deficiency was the motivation for the Scottish story.

CHAPTER THREE:

OVERSEAS EVACUATION

The Evacuation undertaking *within the country* has already comprehensively been outlined. But there was also a significant World War Two Evacuation to some of the British dominions and to the United States of America, which is the subject of this chapter. This undertaking was known as the Children's Overseas Reception Board (C.O.R.B.) and was instrumental in facilitating the transportation of many children 'across the seas' to safe havens at the beginning of the war. The examination of the overseas Evacuation is important because it offers an explanation and understanding of the perceived ease with which many British parents were prepared to part from their children as they travelled to places very far from the United Kingdom.

A History of Child Migration from the United Kingdom
The idea of evacuating children during World War Two to places outside Britain, often unaccompanied, was developed against the backdrop of a long existing period of child migration from Britain to other parts of the world which included Australia, Canada, New Zealand, the then Rhodesias (Northern and Southern) and South Africa. The child migration policies were born of an element of social engineering, essentially to provide labour for the British Empire. It was also from a belief that it was prudent to build a 'sturdy yeomanry' of rural workers, that is, that a life in the country benefitted children from inner city housing environments as espoused by the Fairbridge Farm Schools and the Dr Barnardo's organisations. The policies had been in place

from the 17th century. The child migration schemes continued until the 1970s; however the peak was reached between 1870 and the start of World War One in 1914. Estimates are that at least 100,000 children were sent from Britain during that period under various schemes and political administrations. The schemes were the province of primarily non-government religious and philanthropic organisations. Dr Barnardo's Homes in the United Kingdom is an important example of a facilitator of these schemes (Commonwealth of Australia [*Lost Innocents: Writing the Record, Report of Child Migration*, 2001).

However, that the British did plan and execute the exodus of 1.5 million children from their homes to strange new domiciles often unaccompanied and for long periods of time, needs to be understood in terms of the cultural position of children in the 1930s and their rights and roles. These included the institution and tradition of the boarding school (predominantly in England), to which children were sent from the age of seven (the formative influence for many parliamentarians and civil servants), the transportation of working class children to the colonies, and the apparent ease with which children were placed in orphanages during that period. David Hill (2007, p.xiv), himself a child migrant, notes in the preface to his autobiography:

> Britain is the only country in history to have exported its children. Fairbridge was one of a number of British child-migrant schemes that operated for over a hundred years ... altogether these schemes dispatched about 100,000 under-privileged children – unaccompanied by their parents – to the British colonies, mainly to Canada, Australia and Rhodesia. The child-migrant schemes were motivated by a desire to 'rescue' children from the destitution, poverty and moral danger they were exposed to as part of the lower orders of British Society.

The Australian experience is used as an example of the child migration relationship between Britain and one of its colonies in order to establish the context of the C.O.R.B.

The Australian policy and implementation of wartime Evacuation was an extension of the legacy of child migration from Britain. As noted above, child migration from Britain to Australia had been a feature of British and Australian policy and strategies from Australian Federation in 1901 until World War Two. Financial support had always been forthcoming from both the British and the Australians, but waned during the Depression. Children were deemed to be ideal immigrants by both the sending and receiving countries for perhaps obvious reasons. They were easily controlled, they were acquiescent and did not engender political angst since they were not gainfully employed, and therefore did not pay taxes (Calcott 2001, n.p.). But, as noted above, it was not only governments who embraced the perceived benefits of child migration; many non-government organisations were also active in this scheme. These included the established churches (Anglican, Catholic, Baptist, Methodist, Congregationalist and Presbyterian) as well as organisations such as St Vincent de Paul, the British Women's Overseas League, the British Empire Service League, and as noted before, Dr Barnardo's Homes and Fairbridge Farm Schools. Beyond the formal child migrations schemes, when war was declared in Europe, many voluntary organisations sponsored and assisted refugees or evacuees. In common across all voluntary social organisations, government funding was an important element in the success of the schemes (Calcott 2001, n.p.).

The child migration schemes were established essentially to deal with the abject poverty in some areas of Britain (National Archives.gov.uk: *yourarchives*) and the success of the schemes was deemed to be due largely to the perceived rescue of the children from the social inequality of life in Britain until as late as the 1970s. The autobiography of Hill (2007) tells of the children who found themselves in the Fairbridge Farm School in Pinjarra, Western Australia (Hill 2007). Hill's work charges that the child migrants to Australia were betrayed by the system which allegedly rescued children from 'destitution, poverty and moral danger' as outlined in the Fairbridge pamphlets (Hill 2007, p.4). The Fairbridge experience is the subject of several works, by past Fairbridgians and others, such as Calcott's (2001) anthology of Fairbridge child migrant stories from Southern Rhodesia (now Zimbabwe). During this period, parents from the poorer classes, but mothers in particular, were deemed (and no doubt doomed) to be 'problem mothers'. Indeed as pointed out by Starkey (2000, p.540):

> Eugenic ideas informing the construct of the 'problem mother' determined the ways in which the phenomenon was understood and treatment designed, and contributed to the

failure to develop a critique of the poverty and deprivation which afflicted families. As material conditions improved after the War, so the incidence of the 'problem family' declined, although changing fashions in childcare continued to hold mothers responsible for ills affecting their families.

On 16 November 2009, the then Prime Minister of Australia, Kevin Rudd, apologised on behalf of the country to those, now known as the 'Forgotten Children', who suffered under these various child migration schemes (forgottenaustralianshistory.gov.au). In February 2010, the then British Prime Minister, Gordon Brown, also offered a public apology in this regard (Walker 2009, n.p.). Despite a literature of the appalling experiences endured by some child migrants in existence for up to three decades, it is only in the very recent past that the 'betrayal' of children by previous governments has been acknowledged by current governments.

The Australian Commonwealth report, from which the statistics were accessed for this study, found that, whilst various non-government agencies were eager receivers of child migrants, it was the British government who had the ultimate say regarding the legitimacy of the child migration scheme. This willing approach to separation from family and exile for the children is, suggested to be a serious indictment on the official view of the British child before and subsequent to migration. In common with those of the evacuees' stories, there are differing accounts of their experiences. Indications are that, although many had positive memories, many were also scarred for life (Hill 2007, pp.154-185. That the British establishment had embraced such schemes over such a long period of time no doubt played its part in the acceptance by the wartime powers that the overseas Evacuation policy was a reasonable one, in particular the Evacuation of British children to the then colonies/dominions and unofficially to the United States of America. Indeed, many offers of help from overseas companies, in particular from the United States of America, to harbour British children were made at the beginning of the war, when the possibility of invasion of Britain was a very real prospect. These included American companies such as Kodak, Hoover, Ford and Warner Brothers, employees of which were working in Britain at the onset of war (Henderson 2008, p.96).

The Children's Overseas Reception Board (C.O.R.B.)

It could be argued that a national consequence of the official migration policies developed by Britain and its colonies prior to World War II, was that the colonies would again be prevailed upon to offer sanctuary to children at risk, albeit this time due to the threat of war rather than poverty. However, the C.O.R.B. approach was quite different from other existing child migrant schemes, due to the temporary nature of the Evacuation. The C.O.R.B.'s terms of reference were:

> To consider offers from overseas to house and care for children, whether accompanied, from the European war zone, residing in Great Britain, including children orphaned by the war and to make recommendations thereof (NationalArchives.gov.uk: *yourarchives*).

The plan to send British children to overseas locations was developed as a result of the many offers from those who resided in the then British colonies and dominions to provide a safe haven to the British children, obviating to an extent the need to request such assistance. To this end, the British government made plans to evacuate children outside the country by the establishment of a Children's Overseas Reception Board which arranged for children to be sent to Canada, Australia, New Zealand and South Africa. Overseas Evacuation was formalised on 7 June 1940 by the British government via a quickly assembled committee the remit of which was to consider the offers from overseas. The Board then proceeded to secure places through official means. Issues dealt by the Board included the applications for settlement (both for British children and those resettled in Britain from occupied Europe, North Africa and Asia), sorting, selecting and approving the children, contacting the parents and arranging parties at the ports. Perhaps most importantly, staff from the Board had as a major duty to ensure that correspondence was maintained with the colonies/dominions in particular to ensure a positive approach to the eventual return of the children after the war. Scotland had its own Advisory Council which adhered to the policy developed and required by the London Board. A liaison officer was appointed in order that the Scottish Council would be kept abreast of the daily decisions and progress (NationalArchives.gov.uk: *yourarchives*). The C.O.R.B scheme was differentiated from other schemes which had, over a period of time organised the placement of children abroad, inasmuch as the C.O.R.B. children's exile would be for the duration of the war only.

When the scheme was initiated, it immediately received over 200,000 applications, and this response overwhelmed the Board. The decision to halt further entries was made in early July 1940. Again in common with land evacuees, most of the children who were accepted lived in areas deemed most vulnerable to air attack; some also came from families already split up by Evacuation within Britain (Jackson 2006, Chapter Three). A further 211,000 applications for the Evacuation of children between the ages of 5 and 16, were received subsequent to the Evacuation of Dunkirk (1940) as France fell to Germany (NationalArchives.gov.uk: *yourarchives*). It is interesting to note that the authorities agreed to provide a proportion of on-ship accommodation for Scottish applicants, each sailing party being selected with care to represent a cross-section of society.

The C.O.R.B. scheme resolved that 'for the time being children would not be accompanied by parents but, if possible, special arrangements may be made later for war widows with children' (Palmer 1997, p.75). One of Scottish participants, Janice (from Edinburgh), attests to the extraordinary precepts of the C.O.R.B. scheme:

> *Anyway at the time, my mother had a sister in America and one in Australia and both of them wanted my mother to let me go to them because they believed that we (in Britain) were about to be obliterated by the German bombing. However, my Mother decided that that was not going to happen. I am an only child so very precious to my mother naturally. As it happened the boat that I would have gone on was torpedoed so that was a very good decision on my mother's part.*

Although many children were safely evacuated overseas, the problems related to the transport dangers became insurmountable since it was not possible to release the necessary warships from battle engagement to escort the Evacuation ships. Nevertheless, exit permits for children being sent by private arrangement were still granted so long as parents chose and were able to make private arrangements. Precise statistics are not available, but indications are that 11,000 children went by private arrangement, over 6,000 to Canada and the remainder to the United States (NationalArchives.co.uk).

As Palmer (1997, p.75) notes, the number of children who spent time overseas was swelled by those from the richer classes who chose to and were able to make private arrangements. In total, the government C.O.R.B. despatched 2,664 children who became known as Sea evacuees, over a period of three months. Canada received the bulk of them: 1,532 in nine parties. Three parties sailed for Australia, with a total of 577 children, while 353 went to South Africa in two parties and 202 to New Zealand, again in two parties. A further 24,000 children had been approved for sailing within the three months and over 1,000 escorts, including doctors and nurses, enrolled. At its height, the C.O.R.B. employed some 620 staff (yourarchives.nationalarchives.gov.uk).

Social concerns included citizens' anxiety regarding the exile of young children and separation from their parents and friends. Nevertheless, the schemes were mounted and were open to all, regardless of the financial position of the family. The Board ultimately received more than 400,000 applications on behalf of children whose parents/guardians believed it was in their children's interest to leave Britain. According to Huxley (2008, p.96) the overseas Evacuation had become a political and emotional issue as reports appeared in British newspapers of children of better off families enjoying American and Canadian hospitality, one example:

> Why should the son of the rich man sleep in security in New York's gay lighted towers, the roar of traffic bound on peaceful errands in his ears, while the son of the poor man dozed in crowded shelters below our dangerous cities, menaced by the bomber's drone? It was unfair; and something ought to be done.

As it turned out, the scheme had a short life due to the loss of 77 children's lives in the sinking of a ship, *The City of Benares*, carrying children across the Atlantic in 1940, the *City of Benares*, which was described as follows:

> Four days, 600 miles out to sea, the destroyer HMS *Winchelsea* and two sloops, who had been escorting the

convoy, departed to meet eastbound Convoy HX71. Despite a standing order to disperse the convoy and *et al.* ships proceed on their own, Rear Admiral Mackinnon delayed the order. Shortly after 10pm the City of Benares was torpedoed by Uboat, U-48. The order to abandon City of Benares was given but due to rough conditions and Force 5 winds, lowering the boats was difficult and several capsized. Two hundred and forty five lives were lost either from drowning or exposure. Rescue did not arrive until 14:15 the following afternoon when HMS arrived on the scene and rescued 105 survivors. Only 13 of the children survived, 6 of whom spent seven days in a life boat before being rescued by HMS *Anthony* (NationalArchives. gov.uk n.d./Wartimememories n.d.).

After this tragedy, the government's decision that all convoys carrying civilians would henceforth be accompanied by rescue escorts resulted from this tragedy.

Far Away Lands

Those who went to Australia travelled under the auspices of the wartime children's Evacuation schemes. Those who travelled to America were hosted by employers and friends who volunteered to look after the children for the duration of the war. The Australian contribution is deemed to be of more relevance to this study, due to the colonial ties to Britain as opposed to the American participants' experiences. Further, the British evacuees' evacuations to America were all privately arranged. With regard to the Australian government's offers to host the British children, and the numbers were considerable in the period before and during World War II, the authorities remained selective about the children's country of origin: preference was given to children from Britain, rather than Europe, even though awareness of the atrocities which were being perpetrated in Europe was common knowledge (Palmer 1997, pp.96-97). The accounts of the British children who spent time in Australia as refugees from war torn Europe make an important comparison with the experiences of British children who remained in Britain. In other words, in common with the land evacuees, the children who left to go overseas also spent much of their childhood away from their homes, many without their parents, during

World War II. They experienced similar feelings related to exile as those who remained in their home country, although not in their own homes. They were viewed similarly by the governments of both the United Kingdom and Australia as peripheral to the importance of the troubled times of war (NationalArchives.gov.uk).

Alastair from Lanarkshire, in Scotland, who was evacuated to Regina in Saskatchewan, Canada recalled his experience as a non-government evacuee. Alastair was not accompanied by his mother but by his two brothers. Alastair was 10 years old at the time. His family had deemed Evacuation to be of great importance particularly as the possibility of bombing in Scotland's industrial heartland had increased. Alastair sailed on the S.S. *Cameronia* which was a luxury liner of its time. In Alastair's own words:

> *I wasn't scared about any of it because I was ten and I had a big brother and a younger brother to bother about. We were on our way to stay with close relatives so it was really a bit of an adventure. I do remember my mother telling us she was sad but relieved that even if she didn't survive, we children would. I'm not sure what I think about that now, because I wouldn't have let my children go in any circumstance.*

> *The first place we stayed was in Scourie, near Vancouver, in British Columbia but that didn't last long because this was my mother's cousin and her husband and they had no children and we were presumably a horrendous prospect for them for the duration of the war. This was of course only 1940. I think they were a bit 'straight up and down'. We then moved to Regina in Saskatchewan.*

> *I was a very small child for my age and I recall lots of the Canadian big students taking the mickey out of me, but the teacher (she was Scottish) was very kind and compensated for the children. I attended the local Presbyterian Church and joined the Scouts. We stayed away for four full years but when we went home, my father had had a stroke, so my mother had to go to work at that stage. But he did recover and retained his successful business which was tent-making (the biggest in Scotland).*

We sailed back to the UK on the ship called the Rangitiki joining a convoy out of New York but the ship lost the convoy and we had to go back to New York. We did ultimately get to Liverpool. By the way this was 1944.

Although I had loved being in Canada, I was actually really happy to be home. My brother however joined the Canadian Navy before we left and spent the rest of his life over there. Strange how lives turn out and the causes therefrom.

Unfortunately my father died in 1947 at a very young age. As it turned out I inherited the business and thanks to his hard work (and mine) I am now at an age where I will hand it over to my own son. By the way, I have only told this story to a few people because I have never been interviewed in any formal way. I might add that my immediate family is sick to death of it. But thanks for listening and I hope my experience is of some use to you.

I also interviewed in South Australia an evacuee Allen (originally from Kent) who had been evacuated twice during the war, first to Cornwall and then to America. His detailed recall is absorbing:

My Dad managed a major hotel in London. This was the time of the C.O.R.B. processing and due to the fact that my father was situated in the middle of London in that particular hotel, he knew all that was going on. There was a Colonel who was instrumental in setting up the C.O.R.B. However, that didn't happen for us. Instead in the hotel many bands came to play there and often swapped with US bands and my father got to know one of the managers of a particular band. He suggested to my father that my brother and I should go to the U.S., in fact to California and the next thing on 29 June 1940 we were off on the S.S. Sumeriah. We boys were very confident due to the level of sophistication of my father, no doubt due to his job and we had the best time. One of our most memorable weekends, was when we stayed with some 20 other children, evacuees, at Bob Hope's ranch. Martha Ray and others were there and we were given cowboy suits and stagecoach rides held up

by bad cowboys, marshmallows cooked over a campfire, lassoing ex-
hibitions and the like. The Evacuation did me no harm at all and
made me very independent.

The work of others such as Palmer (1997) and Henderson (2008) whose an-
thologies offer further insights into the experiences of several children who
were evacuated to America and Australia But Grace (from London) recalled:

> I was 12 when I returned to a grey, bomb-damaged London.
> I did not really care for my parents but accepted them as I
> had learned over the last five years to accept everything. For
> my mother, though glad I was safe through the war, it must
> have been hard when I returned and was not the loving seven
> year old she sent away. School was difficult but I coped (Hen-
> derson 2008, pp.93-105),

and as Doreen (Henderson 2008, p.102) who spent some time in Canada, reflected:

> My foster father was a mayor and I don't doubt he felt a cer-
> tain pride in the achievement of the town. There was also
> mental illness in the family, education was out of joint, it was
> an artificial life, and on the whole it was a bad thing we went.

The foregoing narratives again confirm the range of experiences of the overseas evacuees which was similar to those who stayed in the home country.

It can always be suggested of any research such as this, that it is simply a snapshot. However, this small snapshot in no way diminishes the evacuees' contribution to the oral history of their involvement in a very significant undertaking
during World War II.

Two unusual Evacuation experiences are outlined here. One is an interesting
departure from the typical Evacuation to Australia from Britain is the subject
of an autobiography written by Gillian Nikakis (2005, p.205), which tells of
the evacuation of her family from Rabaul in Papua New Guinea in 1942 and
of their subsequent life in Victoria, Australia for the duration of the war. She

makes a similar point to some of those noted above who spent time overseas in as much as her time away from home was a positive experience. Indeed, she ultimately called Australia home.

The other is that of Irene, age 12 when evacuated, who lived in Stanley Prison in Hong Kong in married employees' quarters with three servants. This is the beginning of her story:

> *We had a very comfortable life and from time to time my mother helped out in the prison where my dad was a prison officer. My mother was born in Hong Kong and met my father there. I do recall that my parents had a great social life in Hong Kong. So when war broke out, we were to be evacuated to Australia and the name of the ship was Dos Remedios. This was in 1940. We had British passports but we ended up in Manilla. Actually after Manilla we had as a family intended to go back to Hong Kong but my father decided to stay in Manilla at Port McKinlay at the barracks. I hadn't realised he would stay and was very upset.*

> *When my father came back to Hong Kong in 1941, he unfortunately died of pneumonia in a hospital but I do recall very vividly that on 7 December when I got to school after a visit to the hospital, I heard aeroplanes and they were Japanese.*

Conclusion

This chapter is an important and notable component of the story of the Scottish Evacuation because it sheds light on the prevailing social relationships across the British Empire during the Evacuation period. This is confirmed by the level of support offered by Australia, Canada, South Africa and to a lesser extent, and for different reasons from the United States of America. These relationships have maintained into the 20th century, albeit with a much diminished notion of Empire, now subsumed into the more contemporarily accepted term 'British Commonwealth'. However, as pointed out by Gardiner (2005, pp.78-87) were less inclined to offer to assistance to European families and children.

A background to the origins of child migration to Australia, Canada and Southern Rhodesia has been examined shedding light on the ease with which parents parted from their children to distant regions of the Empire. The findings illustrate that the British not only planned and enabled without great opposition, the Evacuation within the country, but also the movement of children to overseas destinations, due in some part to the British history of child migration. That is, the Evacuation both within and external to the country, met with little public objection and indeed with some enthusiasm. That in times of tumult, colonial host families were willing to extend their homes to young strangers and to give them a safe and rewarding experience confirms the ongoing ties to Britain by the colonies during the period. The findings also suggest that children were more adaptable than realized and that bonds between children and parents can be broken for a time but mended without negative consequences. Contrary to this perception, later research conducted by Heinl (2008), Parsons (2006) and Roman (2008) has acknowledged that trauma can manifest itself negatively many years after the event, as has been the experience of some evacuees.

CHAPTER FOUR:

BUT SCOTLAND IS DIFFERENT

Evacuation Understanding/History

Much of the available literature on the Evacuation is centred on the English experience which tends to imply that the Scottish and English experiences can be subsumed into the 'British' Evacuation. However, it is argued that political and social differences between Scotland and the rest of the United Kingdom underlie some of the differences between the Scottish Evacuation and those of the other parts of the country. This story brings the Scottish experience to light.

Of significance is that not many Scottish evacuees indicated a willingness to be involved in a national ceremonial commemoration of the Evacuation at St Paul's Cathedral in London on 1 September 2009. Through their narratives, they indicated the reasons for their reluctance or lack of interest and from the interviews specific to the event, there emerged the notion that the Evacuation was 'then' and this is 'now' and of little consequence to their lives.

An initial overview of the existing literature suggested that a substantial emphasis is placed on the English child Evacuation experience, and although the Evacuation also took place in Scotland, it is less well documented. The research involved time being spent at both the National Archives of Scotland in Edinburgh and the Kew Library in Richmond, London. The limited primary sources located help to explain the dearth of scholarly inquiry relative to the Scottish Evacuation experience. In the context of the British

Evacuation experience, it is argued that this absence is representative of the general literary and media concentration on England's social and political history to the relative exclusion of Scotland's contemporary history. This of course includes the lack of interest in the Scottish Evacuation story by Scotland's own historical and social agencies. This work/story therefore redresses, at least in part, the lack of formal examination of the Scottish Evacuation story.

An initial critique of a wide range of primary and secondary sources was undertaken, including the literature from which the intended outcomes of this book were developed. This literature includes an analysis of the social, economic and political cultures within Britain during the first half of the twentieth century, which includes the lead up to, and implementation of, the Evacuation policy. These conditions impacted greatly on the decisions, outcomes and implications relative to the Evacuation policy. The participants' oral reflections and the secondary sources complemented each other and allowed the personal narratives and the formal account to be meaningfully connected. The secondary sources provided the factual information which was in turn elicited from the questionnaire. The participants' individual insights enabled the story to develop and most importantly to ensure that their voices were heard: this was an issue close to the heart of many evacuees who felt that their experiences were rather neglected.

A 2004 retrospective edition of the *Evening Times*, a popular Glasgow evening newspaper, offers a 'story in pictures' of the evacuation exodus across Scotland as the evacuees were entrained on their way to a sojourn with no guarantees beyond their arrival in a place quite different from home (*Evening Times 2004*).

From this retrospective, it was confirmed understood that most of the *government* evacuees came from backgrounds that the interviewees in this study described as 'ordinary' or suggested 'were all the same'. While in much of the literature the assumption was made that these descriptors translated to an impoverished existence, this was not the view of the Scottish evacuees of this study, although many came from the more industrial areas of the major cities where the housing was sometimes of a poorer standard relative to the middle class of the time. As Calder (1969, p.29) confirms of the post-World War One era:

> In the New Britain, the immigrant worker from Scotland and his manager, perhaps only recently arrived in the middle class by a daring ascent of the flimsy educational ladder, danced to the same tunes and watched the same films ... the old ideology of laissez faire which had served the British ruling class so well has been on its last legs.

It is difficult to argue that there was a typical evacuee in that they did not form a homogeneous group. They were nevertheless a unique group since, although they were part of the war, they saw no action either in the theatre of war or in their homes away from home. This conflicting situation was the subject of much contemplation by the participants during the interviews. In this regard, the research has revealed some major surprises and contradictions.

The recording of the stories of the children of war and exile is a relatively recent phenomenon (Parsons 1998), confirming that no account of any war experience could be complete without hearing from the children. Without their contribution, a crucial dimension of the human experience is lost as well as the loss of an opportunity to assist the healing process for the children who experienced harm during their exile, as in the case of some of the evacuees. Since I essentially see this social enquiry as a story, it was initially rather daunting to try to encapsulate it completely in academic terms. I was inspired by Robyn Annear (2008, p.4), who reflects thus on her initial success:

> I was aware of a bit of disapproval from the academy that I had got away with something and I was told I was a postmodernist, which I had to learn a bit about, but I'm not a historian, I'm a story teller.

The extent to which the historian has a role as story teller may be a subject of debate, but undoubtedly the historian is a detective as Paul Ham (2008, p.4) in the same article says:

> ... one of the primary qualifications for a historian is the love of and delight in research. There's a frisson that runs down your spine when you sight something in a document that no one has seen before you.

Comfort was taken from both of these successful writers who appear to share the desire to write history that is accessible to the general reader, without lacking academic rigour.

CHAPTER FIVE:

SMALL NATION AND BIG NATION

This theory of the Small Nation and the Big Nation is of great significance to this story. It is important because the theory (and practice) indicates that philosophies, histories and cultures of small nations juxtaposed against big nations (who share the same language) are often less well acknowledged and sometimes ignored completely. This part of the chapter examines the theory in order to ascertain the ease with which the small nation's history and culture can be subsumed into those of their *bigger* next door neighbour, and then are inevitably articulated from the perspective of the big nation. In this case, the small nation is Scotland and the big nation is England.

The relativities between the small nation and the big nation are well illustrated when considering other obvious examples. These include America and Canada; Germany and Austria; and Australia and New Zealand. These countries share a common language and a common border (in the case of Australia and New Zealand, the Tasman Sea), as opposed to other examples, such as Sweden/Norway and Spain/Portugal, which, whilst sharing a common border, do not share a common language. Language differentiation itself ensures a global recognition. However, as stated above, in instances in which a small nation has both a common language and is physically juxtaposed with the big nation, the small nation invariably suffers from a lesser profile and relevance in a global sense than its more prominent neighbours. An example of a similar viewpoint relative to Canada and the United Stated is described by Shields (2008, p.93):

When Cuyler Goodwill speaks, as he often does these days, about 'living in a progressive country' or 'being a citizen of a proud free nation' he is referring to the United States of America and not to the Dominion of Canada, where he was born and where he grew to manhood. Canada with its forests and lakes and large airy spaces lies now on the other side of the moon as does the meagreness of its short, chilly history. There are educated Bloomingtonians - he meets them every day who have never heard of the province of Manitoba, or if they have, they're unable to spell it correctly or locate it on a map. They think Ottawa is a town in south-central Illinois, and that Toronto lies somewhere in the northern counties of Ohio. It's as though a huge eraser has come down from the heavens and wiped out the top of the continent.

This considered quote might assist in providing an explanation for the lack of interest, historical or social, in the Scottish Evacuation, which is puzzling since the Scottish Evacuation was proportionately as comprehensive as the undertaking in England. That is, the smaller nation, in insisting of a profile for itself can be viewed by the larger nation as vexatious, rather than simply as a plea for acknowledgement and recognition of its distinctiveness. This view is confirmed by Heffer (2009, p.17) when he states his abhorrence of the notion of Scottish independence thus:

> ... the subsidy from other parts of the Kingdom [ie England] to Scotland is currently at least 22 billion pounds a year. If Mr Salmond [the First Minister of Scotland] and his friends have long been able to contemplate independence while trying to work out an alternative source of income to replace that subsidy ... that to delay an independence referendum ... would also mean that the nightmare of actually having to govern a seriously poor country like Scotland could be postponed for a further while yet.

Whilst the Evacuation policy was applied *similarly* in both countries, this dissertation has revealed that several significantly different experiences and outcomes are evident. To subsume the Scottish Evacuation experience into that of the English one, serves only to illustrate neglect of the small nation's relevance, not only with regard to the Evacuation and its planning, but potentially also with regard to many other political and identity issues.

An important example of a less well documented major event, which took place in Scotland in 1941: the Clydebank Blitz, was proportionately as horrendous as the bombing of Coventry in England, yet is often omitted from World War Two histories (MacPhail 19740, p.94)[6]. As Linklater (2010, p.29) points out in his review of Gardiner's 2010 book *The Blitz: the British under attack:*

> Traditionally the Luftwaffe's bombing campaign used to be termed the London Blitz, as though only the capital was involved. It is worth bearing in mind, therefore, that between September 1940 and May 1941 when Hitler's invasion of Russia brought the bombing to an end, more than half the deaths, 23,000 out of a total of 43,000, with almost two-thirds of the buildings destroyed, approaching two of the three million, and perhaps four-fifths of the manufacturing capacity put out of action *outside of London..*

This observation substantiates the hypothesis that the public imagination outside of Scotland confers upon it the notion that Scotland is simply another region of England, specifically in this story, regarding the Evacuation, but there are many other examples.

Exclusion

The English or national ambivalence during and beyond World War Two regarding Scotland's place in the country (the United Kingdom) are outlined hereunder.

In the following examples the actual word 'Scotland' is often excluded from the British lexicon when discussing the United Kingdom. This exclusion at the time of the Evacuation and writing about its history is demonstrated in works of writers such as Titmuss (1950), Holman (1995), and Wicks (1988) who allude to the situation in Scotland only perfunctorily. To omit the other nations in much of the British Evacuation literature and debate indicates that the small nation is less relevant than the big nation to many historians and other scholars.

The most recent relevant example is that of the commemoration service which took place on 1 September 2009 at St Paul's Cathedral, London. On the day, the Reverend Hugh Ellis in his address suggested that both 'England and Germany' suffered similar fates with regard to the children of war. The exclusion of the evacuees from other parts of the United Kingdom was/is very disappointing and troubling and confirms that the big nation is still regarded as pre-eminent ever as recently as 2009.

However, earlier concerns regarding this omission surfaced at the time of the Evacuation: an example is that given by Calder (1969, p.33):

> When Chamberlain appeared in the House of Commons that evening, its members expected him to announce war. Instead, his speech seemed to foreshadow a second Munich. As Arthur Greenwood, acting Labour leader during the illness of Clement Attlee, rose to reply, little Leo Amery, a veteran Tory imperialist and confirmed anti-appeaser, shouted 'Speak for England, Arthur'. Other Conservatives, ashamed at this temporizing, took up the call, and from the Labour benches came cries of 'Speak for the workers' and 'Speak for Britain', a pertinent reminder that Scotland and Wales were also involved.

Rose (2003, p.220) also notes that:

> In June 1941 Scottish complaints about how the nation was often named reached the House of Commons. A Scottish Labour MP submitted a written question to the Prime Minister suggesting that when Government ministers and other officials used 'England' for Britain', they 'cause hurt to Scotland, and Northern Ireland, *[whither Wales?]* and the other lands of our common people, who are together in the one purpose and spirit'. The Prime Minister ... saw 'no necessity for any further special directions' to ministers and the BBC

concerning the precise 'meanings of the terms England, Scotland, and Britain'.

Further examples regarding the omission of the small nation's history or stories can be found in the work of Gardiner and others, most recently in 2010 as noted above. Gardiner (2005) in her chapter on the Evacuation does not include a single anecdote of a Scottish evacuee's experience. However, accounts of the *Kindertransport*, the Jewish children evacuated from Germany and Austria to Britain, and of the Basque children escaping the Nationalist bombing during the Spanish Civil War, are given considerable prominence. Similarly, Hall (1998, p.29) in her discussion of national identity and its construction, alludes to the notion of the nation's and nations' (in the British context) fascination with the past. To this end, she suggests that history in Britain is essentially about Englishness but momentarily remembers that if Britain is being discussed, then it is not only England.

Hall further suggests that history and national identity are actually about days of empire and hegemony and some place 'untouched by capitalist relations or exploitation' (Hall 1998, p.30). She continues her confused treatise of what it means to be British by the complete omission of Scotland. This confusion is compounded by her suggestion that memory work needs to be undertaken to take account of the *real* history of nations, making the point that until African-Americans and white Americans can recover the history of slavery and injustice their history is not liveable for the present.

Hall uses the metaphor of Meeropol's seminal poem 'Strange Fruit' to confirm these injustices against African-Americans (2008, p.23). Although taking the moral high ground on behalf of the colonies, it is suggested that Hall herself is guilty of not taking account of the 'real history' of the British nation by neglecting to acknowledge that while Scotland, Northern Ireland and Wales are part of *British* history, they are *not English*. It is therefore suggested that Scotland, Northern Ireland and Wales have no obligation to re-remember the history of the British Empire if it is only to be re-worked as representative of Englishness.

The assumption that the English Evacuation solely represents the British Evacuation is the case in point. Hall is, of course, remonstrating generally with those who offer a false representation of history and many nations are guilty of this transgression. Unfortunately, her own view of the nation state is flawed when she excludes Scotland, Wales and Northern Ireland from her consideration of the constitution of the United Kingdom (of Great Britain and Northern Ireland). Again the big nation prevails to the exclusion of the smaller ones.

Further examples illustrate the dilemma within the United Kingdom relative to the four nationalities/cultures and their place in the country. In this regard, Rose (2003) offers an insightful reflection on the issue of Britishness as it relates to the nations other than England, which make up the United Kingdom. However, while *she* acknowledges that England is only one part of the island (with particular regard to the lead up to and the war years) this research indicates that this understanding was rarely foregrounded by important communication agencies, such as the British Broadcasting Corporation (BBC) during the war/Evacuation period. Indeed, reports written by the *Glasgow Herald*, suggest that media concentration on the English world, whether intentional or otherwise, was profound. 'England' was often used when 'Britain' was the accurate terminology. This practice occurred to the great annoyance of the Scots (and the Welsh), but it appears that this fell on deaf ears because, as the *Glasgow Herald* reported on 24 September 1939:

> the English-men's use of the words "English" and "England" for "British" "Britain" is perfectly consonant with English behaviour in every branch of our common life', and 'in times like these every effort should be made to unite all peoples under the British flag - beginning at home. At the present moment the English are doing their level best to cause disruption on the home front by the careless misuse of the aforementioned term,

and as Calder (1969, p.57) elegantly reflected:

> But even at this stage only the most literal-minded *Englishman* could have believed that he had gone to war for Poland. The *nation*, at last was fighting against Hitler.

As noted above, there are many examples of the assumption that all of the United Kingdom is in fact England but perhaps the most anachronistic is the *British Act of Succession*, which, while banning Catholics from the throne, also declares that the monarch must be in communion with the Church of England, thereby excluding any Presbyterian, the national church in Scotland (Dyer 2000, n.p.).

To illustrate further that the United Kingdom is not England, it is important to note that Scotland has engineered many initiatives independently of the rest of the United Kingdom. For example, Scotland's education system has since its inception been organised quite differently from that of England. The traditional Scottish approach, that of teaching and study of moral philosophy inherent in the Scottish system was a major influence on the planning of new universities across the United Kingdom in the early twentieth century (Lowe 2003, p.324). Lowe further notes that in the early twentieth century the English education system was slow to develop into a national system, in contrast to that of Scotland. In particular, Lowe gives an account of the importance of the impact of ex-patriot Scots who studied in English institutions and contributed to the development of policy there. He suggests that the characteristics of the Scottish system and their profound influence on its English counterparts were of more consequence than the influence of any other nation on England at that time.

Indeed, Scotland's history of universal provision of public education was a forerunner in Europe and to this end, a school was established in every parish in Scotland in 1696 (*the Union of the Crowns* was already 93 years old) by an Act of Scotland's then parliament. This act was known as the *Act for Setting Schools* and required each parish to supply a 'commodious house for a school', and to pay the teacher a salary of no fewer than a hundred marks (then Scottish currency) and no more than two hundred. By the end of the 18th century, Scotland's literacy rate was the highest in the world (Herman 2001, pp.22-23). Although the established church had a vested interest in the literacy of its children, reading of the bible being one of its aims, the ability to read at such an early period in Scotland's social history, furthered an appetite for reading in general among later generations of Scottish children (Herman, 2001, p.24).

Finally, as Haesly (2005, pp.65-83) argues, in contemporary times, the smaller nations of Scotland and Wales have declared their dissonance relative to the British *imagined* community – the notion constructed by Anderson (1991, p.9). Rather, they see themselves as having been marginalised by the big nation over a considerable period of time. Haesly (2005, pp.65-83) suggests that the major political parties in the Westminster parliament have been reluctant to acknowledge that it is necessary to recognise the different socio-political environments of the smaller nations. Such recognition would render legitimacy in the wider context of the United Kingdom, an outcome necessary for the dignity and credibility of all smaller nations.

Disappointingly, with regard to the Scottish Evacuation, the Scots have somewhat neglected their own specific Evacuation story and this is confirmed by the omission of any reference to the Scottish Evacuation in works, for example, by Mackie (1982), Lynch (1992), MacPhail (2000) and Fulton (1999). The first three authors are historians of Scotland whose work includes reflections of World War Two. Fulton's work is an autobiography of his life in Glasgow and other parts of Scotland and his life story includes the period of World War Two. Scotland's literary community must bear responsibility for their own neglect of this important event, now remedied by this account.

This work posits that Scotland's child evacuee history has been neglected, and that this neglect has arisen partly through the 'small nation, big nation' phenomenon, in which the 'small nation' (in this case Scotland) is subsumed into the 'big nation' (England). It is therefore argued that the history of Scotland is important and relevant to the overarching story of the Scottish child Evacuation as it relates to the whole story of the British child Evacuation during World War Two.

This brief history of Scotland has been outlined in order to contextualise the Scottish Evacuation story alongside that of the other British Evacuation. The short account can enable the reader to learn, remember or acknowledge that the Scots have a sense of their own identity, that Scotland's history is an exciting and at times trenchant one and with its own lineage of rulers. It has been argued that significant differences in approach and outlook, both socially and politically between the nations of Scotland and England justify an individual treatment of the Scottish Evacuation experience. These differences include the approach to education, the prevalence of Presbyterianism, the 'state' religion of Scotland and Scotland's left of centre political persuasion.

Ignoring these differences can lead to assumptions being made that the small nation's values, beliefs and aspirations are analogous to those of the big nation, resulting in an absence of historical accounts of Scottish experiences of child evacuees: in other words that to offer a specific account of the Scottish Evacuation was unnecessary.

Of course, in 2014, the support for an Independent Scotland was tested by the Independence Referendum which has energised the debate and the power of the Scottish National Party which will be tested in the British General Election: May 2015.

CHAPTER SIX:

A CHILD OF THE SCOTTISH EVACUATION

Children live in a world of giants, under the existential necessity of extracting reasonably reliable meanings from the giants' riddling speech and baffling conduct (Glendinnen 2008)

Who knows the thoughts of a Child? (Perry 1994)

The fact that many mothers accompanied their children to their 'billets' is of prime importance to the Scottish evacuees' experiences. That is, from the following interview outcomes – most of which are positive – it is acknowledged that the presence of the mothers was crucial to the wellbeing of the Scottish evacuees. This accompaniment by mothers was not the case in most of the English Evacuation experiences. This goes some way to confirm the several dissimilar social policy between Scotland and England at that time which prevail in 2015. Current examples are those of free tertiary education and several 'free health services such as prescription medicine in Scotland.

Who is a Child?
The United Nations defines a child as 'every human being below the age of eighteen years unless under the law applicable to the child, majority is attained earlier' (*Convention on the Rights of the Child* 1990). But, although all states of the United Nations General Assembly are signatories to the Convention, in practice many differing redactions of the definition of a child exist, depending

on a country's economy, social infrastructure, history, costs of labour and other factors. If a country is poor, children are often viewed as consumers, commodities and liabilities, as well as contributors and, although valued when contributors, have tended to be considered as peripheral to mainstream politics. If a country is rich, children are often viewed as consumers of commodities, albeit also considered as peripheral to mainstream politics. However, Gunter and Furnham's work (1998) illustrates that post-war, children in the developed world are increasingly targeted as consumers due to the overall financial and social prosperity experienced from the 1950s.

How then did the British understand the notion of the child from the Victoria era until the end of World War II? In Victorian and Edwardian Britain, working class children were primarily regarded as objects, not subjects, because their value was primarily economic. Employers benefited because children were cheap to employ and often parents were complicit in the exploitation for complex and perhaps defendable reasons. These reasons were a result of high unemployment of parents at several periods during the late 19th and early 20th centuries, and also due to a very strict relief system which did not define able bodied male skilled workers as legitimate recipients of assistance (Knox n.d.) In this case, if children could augment the income of the family, the perception was that, given to no other option, to sell their labour was acceptable. *The Poor Law* of 1868 made it a criminal offence to wilfully neglect a child under fourteen years of age. Neglect was defined as that which would threaten or result in serious injury to a child's health, but there was little incentive to prosecute the perpetrators, because the reality was that if prosecutions were successful, those children would then become a burden on the state. The welfare of the child was therefore of somewhat limited importance. The National Society for the Prevention of Cruelty to Children was formed in response to the 1906 and 1908 *Child Cruelty Acts*. The work of the society benefited from the legislation and became more effective in tackling child neglect and cruelty. The Children's Branch of the Home Office in 1923 stated:

> The children of the poorest classes are better cared for than they used to be and it is now unusual to see dirty and ragged children in the streets of our great cities. Cases of extreme brutality, which were all too common not so many years ago, are becoming less frequent (cited in Rose 1991, p.243).

As late as 1913, although the Children's Charter of 1908 had been implemented, rights of children were scarcely recognised by the governing classes and the notion that a child had any legal rights was viewed as inconceivable (Rose 1991). Pilcher's interest (2007) is the relationship between child development and health education in Britain during the 20th century and much of her work is focussed generally on the development of children and their place in an adult world. Pilcher (2007, p.216) suggests that the 'agency (of children) is framed and conditioned by adult-dominated sets of knowledge, practices and policies'. In particular, she argues, it was to the poorer working class children that government policies and practices were targeted. This targeting, in Scotland, was intended to ensure the future health and progress of the nation and its security according to Devine and Finlay (1996).

Although, as in any war conflict, the place of children is peripheral to the mainstream politics and policies, the choices of the children of the Evacuation were also of limited consequence when compared with the decisions of others, in this case those of their parents or guardians, the political decision makers and the Evacuation administrators. In the case of the evacuated children, they were expected at times to be both a child and an adult. As Nancy (from Glasgow) recalled:

> *Yes, I went to Killin Primary and travelled by bus. I remember this quite clearly. My brother and I had to walk to the main road through the glen. I suppose this was not something I would have been expected to do in the city, but I was actually happy to 'tramp' to school, but any change in routine for a child is great. I think we felt quite 'grown up'.*

Agnes (from Glasgow near Clydebank) also reflected on 'being grown up':

> *It was a huge house, but when we were in the Manse, it was all dark and dreary. Miss Haugh was the house-keeper, and she was not very nice and a bit scary, all dressed in black. There were 16 of us in the Commander's place, and they had maids who were actually sisters: they were like a pantomime. We were treated well, sometimes like children, and then at other times, we had to help in the running of the house with certain duties with a bit of*

responsibility. So the idea of being a child often morphed into being a responsible adult; interesting reflection when you make me think of that now.

The reflections of Nancy and Agnes suggest that at times they were able to behave like children but at other times they were given some level of responsibility either for themselves or for the general household. But although the children of the Evacuation had their own notion of themselves, there was of course an acknowledged place and definition of a child which, over time, evolved. Again, this work by necessity derived much of the evacuation history from the British historical experience with limited concession to the Scottish experience.

The Value of a Child
The latter half of the 19th and the early 20th century places the poor working class children in a rather miserable situation. Education of British working class children, although compulsory, was often more of a health hazard than an enlightenment, due to the poor physical conditions of buildings as well as lack of provision of food, exercise and primitive sanitary conditions (Rose 1991, pp.148/149). Given that the value of children during this period was economic, and that their education was largely perfunctory, the worth of children until the end of the 19th century was markedly different from that of contemporary times. But comprehensive improvements began to be made in the education sector in the late 19th and the first quarter of the 20th century. However, Hopkins argues that these improvements were developed less out of consideration for the child than because of the need for youth training to defend the British colonies and assist in the expansion of the Empire (1994, p.6).

Conversely the children of the professional middle and upper classes in Britain (predominantly male and in England) were being groomed for leadership via the elitist private school system, where pupil boarding was the norm, and which functioned as an institution lying at the heart of the British establishment. Therefore many children of the governing upper classes – again in England, from the late 18th century onwards, spent much of their childhood away from their parents. This separation became accepted as character building, developing leadership ability to be translated to a 'natural right to govern'. The anthology of working childhood experiences by Seabrook (1982) epitomises the history of the social relationships in the British family.

From a largely ignored existence until the late 19th century to the contemporary central position in Western society, children's lives are explored by the writer by narrative discourse. Scotland too has several private elitist educational establishments but far fewer than in England, taking account of both populations. It is therefore argued that the greater number of accompanying mothers in the Scottish Evacuation experience was a reflection of the difference between England and Scotland in the attitude to the provision of private often boarding school, education (*The Scottish Government*:scotland.gov.uk). In other words, there was a prevailing notion that separation from family was acceptable in many parts of England.

As a result of the Evacuation, the establishment view of evacuees was that of a group with no individuality and limited identity; but in fact, on examination of their experiences, it was evident from the participants albeit looking back over a long period of time, that as children they were wise, considered and differentiated. As Isobel (from Glasgow), a participant evacuated at the age of 10, told me in answer to whether or not she believed the Evacuation was necessary:

> *I don't think it was a reasonable thing now, but I suppose we were told it was for our own safety, so at the time I suppose people accepted that. Don't forget we were children and in those days children didn't have much say in anything. I have often wondered if something like what happened to the evacuees could happen today. Children today are much more able to say what they think and are treated much more like people, if you know what I mean.*

> *Children's opinions are listened to and they are allowed to tell their mum and dad what they do and don't like to eat for example. The mums and dads nowadays actually ask what they would like to do, how they are getting on at school, do they like their teacher.*

> *Children today are really independent, but I suppose we were in some ways, like we used to go on public transport ourselves and away we would go in the summer on our bikes – a gang of us – miles away from home.*

Agnes (from Glasgow) recalled when asked if she visited her hosts after the war:

> *Yes I did, lots of time. When I got married my husband and I often visited and we were made very welcome. When I went back with my brother he got to visit his old room. We were treated very well as if we were quite important even though we were only children at the time* [the Evacuation]. *That would have been quite unusual I think.*

These narratives illustrate a level of ambivalence regarding the multifaceted notion of the child, not only from the adult world, but as the evacuees saw themselves. On the one hand, the children of the Evacuation were quite independent of adults as they ventured sometimes unsupervised in their local surroundings. But on the other, they were totally at the behest of authority whose decisions were imposed arbitrarily in the policy development and application of the Evacuation. In due course, however, they were obliged to behave, and did indeed behave, as young adults. This was due to their level of maturity and acute rationale as they understood their situation and the expectations of them by the adult world. This notion is developed further as the chapter unfolds.

Upon examining the literature in the 21st century on the place of, and respect for, children in Britain, the volume is immense relative to the issues of education, health, mental health, gender, justice, and sport among others. In contemporary Britain, children occupy a quite different place from that occupied by their forebears where trauma is now acknowledged (United Nations Convention on the Rights of the Child 1989). As John (from Clydebank) whose recollection was typical of many, when reflecting on his own and his friends' Evacuation experience, recalled:

> *They all seemed to accept what had happened. They were completely different times. Fewer than fifty percent came back to where they lived before the Evacuation* [due to the Clydebank Blitz]. *We didn't talk a lot about it I think even if we had suffered trauma. At that time though, we were just viewed as children, but we were really adults in our behaviour, otherwise we would not have managed.*

In order to comprehend and reflect on how it was to be a Scottish evacuee, aspects of the literature on childhood in different times and in different places have been interrogated. Awareness of significant events such as conflict and outbreaks of disease which have created imperatives in the behavior and roles of children has also proved to be significant.

The chapter includes the notion of the child in the periods leading to and subsequent to World War II: the standards of education; ambiguity in relation to authority, an important component of which was the established church; how the concept of the child has been constructed; the ability to manipulate the child; children's rights as they have developed nationally and internationally; how the British understood the role and place of a child and the social conditions of the evacuees.

Although the place and the notion of the child is the subject of much contemporary research, Plumb (1975) and de Mause (1988) suggested that there had been a regrettable lack of interest by historians relative to children generally in the two centuries prior to World War Two. Nevertheless, both acknowledged the growing academic focus on the child of World War Two and beyond which is confirmed by the abundant literature sourced in this story. One example of a contemporary historical enquiry is *The International Journal of Evacuee and War Child Studies*, which presents the opportunity to acknowledge the research relative to the war child, not only in Britain but also internationally (Kaven 2006, pp.67-70). To characterise any child is a complex undertaking but to characterise the child of the Evacuation in the overall context of how children have been perceived by different cultures and eras, offers a significant challenge.

However, the narratives which facilitate an understanding of the Scottish participants' experiences are the definitive focus of the chapter as they relate to the notion of the Scottish child of the Evacuation. Whilst the literature of the historical and psychological view of the child contextualises the arguments, what is important is that the chapter allows the participants to shape and articulate their views of their childhood during the Evacuation. This study of the Scottish children of the Evacuation era includes the influence of the established churches as well as the social conditions prevailing at the time of the Evacuation. It is important to encapsulate these conditions because the

Evacuation did draw attention to the unequal access to goods and services by Scotland's urban working class compared with other social classes.

The Evacuation thereby provided the opportunity to the policy makers during the late period of the war and beyond, to analyse the causal factors of the social and economic plight of the working classes, and in turn to offer remedies which focused, in Scotland, on structural, rather than behavioural reform (McCrae 2003, p.474).

Scotland at the Time

Scotland during World War Two had many social problems, but the economic and social conditions were paradoxical. On the one hand, Scotland had near full employment during the period of the Evacuation due to the demand for the products of the heavy industries which were the fabric of much of Scotland's economic life. These industries included those of the shipbuilding and steel manufacture. On the other hand, Scotland unfortunately could also boast a serious level of domestic overcrowding. According to the Parliamentary Debates (5th Series cited in Stewart and Welshman 2006), 22.6% of Scottish families lived in overcrowded circumstances, compared with 3.8% in England. Since the state was the main provider of housing during the period of the Evacuation, it was therefore limited due to its level of flexibility to address differentiated needs.

With regard to the Evacuation, this overcrowding (higher household numbers) had resulted in a great demand for the limited number of available billets in the country areas. It also exacerbated the claims by the hosts that they were appalled by the poor health and social conditions, including clothing and footwear, of many of the evacuees – although disputed by the evacuees in this story. This had resulted in an initial hostile response from those who had offered their homes in the country and it is possible that the evacuees might well have been the object of this disapproval (Titmuss 1950, p.36). These claims in due course gave rise to a suggested rural/urban divide readily appropriated by some newspapers, including *The Glasgow Herald* (23 May 1939, n.p.) which noted: 'Rural districts may refuse further evacuees'. Nevertheless, as of the 1931 Scottish census (none was conducted in 1941), there had been a drift to the country areas in Scotland over the previous 20 years from 1911 (A Vision of Britain.org.uk). However, in 1939 and beyond, the rural population centres had remained relatively small and held great appeal for the young evacuees who were enchanted by their new found space. The environs of their new home must have appeared empty to some as Meg (from Glasgow) recalled:

> *We were evacuated to Dumfries in the south of Scotland and we ended up in a place we would normally never have been, especially having a maid! We sat around for a while and then a farmer 'picked' us the whole family. Nevertheless, it was a special experience and we all learned from it I suppose. I have good memories of my time away in the countryside with all that space with hardly anything or anybody in it; not something we were used to, no not at all.*

For their own Good

There is no doubt, however, that the Evacuation was always well intentioned, and it is suggested that the children of the Evacuation, due to the necessity to understand and accept the implementation of processes which were often disadvantageous for them, were not wholly disempowered as sometimes imagined. Rather these children's ability to reason and rationalise a situation was often one of great maturity. Bobbie (from Glasgow) confirms this ability in his candid response to the question 'How did the host family treat you?'

> *Well there was a mum and dad and two boys. They were about 10 and 12 years of age and I was 10 and my brother was eight and my Mum was probably about the same age as the woman who took us in. I'm surmising that. Anyway the house was a big stone thing which looked huge but in fact it didn't have that many rooms. Anyway the three of us got one and we all got on very well. We went to the same school as the boys and settled in fine. We were away for about a year but my mother told us later she got fed up sharing the kitchen. But we did go back to visit them so they must have treated us well. Don't forget Lanark is not that far from the East End of Glasgow where I was reared. To be honest I don't remember thinking much about the house compared with our own*

or the Evacuation actually. We shared bedrooms in my own house anyway. The Evacuation didn't impact much on my life I must say inasmuch as it wasn't sad or scary or anything.

Davie (from Glasgow) had this to say in his overall synopsis of his Evacuation experience:

My sister and my mother and I went to a tenement flat in Ardrossan just like the one we lived in in Glasgow. We had one big room to share again just like we had in Glasgow. The couple whose house it was were OK but because they were much older than my Mum, she told me later it wasn't the happiest time for her trying to keep us quiet etc. I suppose they must have been retired. Still, it was by the sea and my sister and I had great fun and of course since it's just a few miles away from Glasgow, we often have a chuckle about it all. At the time, we thought it was soooo far away.

Bobbie's and Davie's reflections confirm their philosophical attitude towards their experiences: that there was nothing untoward about their time away from home. Again, their happy time while away might have been largely due to the presence of their mother.

By contrast, Ken (from Dagenham), who went to Salcome, did not have the same positive school experience:

It wasn't very nice at school actually because we were treated differently from the other children because we were evacuees. Sometimes we were humiliated because they mimicked our pronunciation. There were other things too, like not having our Mum and Dad to talk to about things. That was a huge issue for our development on reflection. Instead of making me independent, it served to make me a bit insecure. When I went back to Dagenham, the children mimicked my Devon accent!

Again, the importance of having an accompanying parent was apparent in Ken's story.

The participants experienced the normality of happiness as well as sadness regarding the Evacuation which some saw as an exciting adventure of independence and proof of growing up. They also acknowledged that they understood the necessity for the policy of Evacuation inasmuch as their reactions to the fears and dislocation were disarmingly rational. Jenks' sociological view of the adult: normal, natural and rational, also has application for the child. Jim (from Clydebank) told me:

> *Well, it wasn't unhappy for me because my mother was with us; we had the kindest people around us and we had all this space and freedom. I sometimes wonder what it would have been like to have experienced the Blitz on my home town. I mean, I suspect I would have been a bit excited at all the carnage etc. Sounds daft, but I think that's how I would have felt. Still, how lucky we were to have such an experience which has stayed with me forever. We have been back a few times to 'have a look' because as you know, nowhere is far in Scotland!*

Isobel (from Glasgow) shared Jim's sentiments when she recalled decisions made and her philosophical view of them:

> *I was ten years old. My Evacuation came about because of the bombing of Clydebank. The first night of the blitz we were all rushed out of the building and we ran up to Maryhill Park which was nearby. To make us feel safer, we armed ourselves with tin washing up basins which we held over our heads. It seems pretty daft now as the park housed a detachment of search lights and ack-ack guns and barrage balloons! The second night my father refused to leave the flat because he thought he was safer in his bed. A wise man, my father. We ended up not too far away from Clydebank which seems a bit daft now, but what would I have known then?*

Isobel at the interview thought the issue of the tin washing up basins held over her head was 'daft', but she suggested that she understood the importance of the decision of her father very clearly at the time.

The Evacuees'/Children's War Too

World War II, in many respects, was the children's war as well as the adult war: the loss of an important part of their childhood impacted on them as much as the loss by the adults of their freedom to choose their everyday life's activities and pursuits. This loss of childhood was manifested in the severing of family bonds which were sometimes not able to be re-established. As recalled earlier by Alastair, his father died in 1947 when he had to grow up very quickly. Gardiner's (2005) observation that some of the children also experienced feelings of rejection and loneliness is confirmed by Betty (from Clydebank):

> *The people in the Dunoon* [Scottish seaside resort] *house were just a couple, but I remember they made us feel quite bad as if we shouldn't be there or something. It took me a long time to understand that they got paid to house us! But I think we just had to put up with it. My mum was really sad about it all, but she didn't really show that until we talked about it all much later. Stoic we were.*

As Pat (from Dagenham) recalled:

> *I was homesick all the time and again I was always feeling hurt that my parents didn't visit in all that time.* [Participant weeps]: *sorry about that; and yet my Mum was a very gentle woman. But of course it was wartime and everything was different. But how I longed for her.*

Jack (from Glasgow), whose parents were deaf and dumb, when considering whether or not he thought the Evacuation was necessary, had thoughts similar to those of Pat inasmuch as they had become inextricably bound to the war effort.

> *I suppose that because the bombing had already started and we were all aware of it, that my parents thought it was the obvious thing to do. Don't forget in those times, people didn't challenge officialdom as much as they do now. Also, the deaf and dumb aspect was an important one. What I mean is, although they might have understood the importance of an official Evacuation process, I'm not sure they would have gone along with us being moved to a strange place with*

strange people. But my mother and father managed to come to see us quite often and how wonderful was that.

Although the children and parents of the Evacuation suffered from their dislocation and disconnection, they appeared to have understood that it was for their own good and therefore acquiesced often without demur. Again, according to Pat (from Dagenham):

Nobody was really bothered about the children. According to my mother everyone was pleased to see us back, but I don't remember anybody saying welcome back to us children. We just got on with it. Those were the days of seen and not heard eh?

Margaret (from Clydebank) expressed similar feelings:

Well it was fine of course because although we were away from home for most of the war, we were not that far away from Clydebank (our home town). But we didn't have any means of getting there so it was a bit strange it would only be about 10 miles from where we were to Clydebank but I am only questioning this now. I didn't at the time.

Pat's and Margaret's observations indicate both discernment and sense of disempowerment, as well as helping us to understand how complex a child's understanding can be and indeed a child's acceptance, of a situation. This theme, that the evacuees were very clear that the Evacuation was for their own good, was reiterated many times in the narratives. This does not mean that this edict was not questioned. It means that for a time they were prepared to accommodate this concept. This theme is echoed again and again as Gordon (from Glasgow) confirms:

Well, I think my parents were sort of persuaded that it was a good thing to protect your children, but it was a bit of a strange thing really when you think about. Because they were persuaded, we just had to go along with it, and to be honest, I didn't even think about protesting. I suspect today's children would though. Nevertheless, it was a special experience, and we all learned from it, I suppose. I have good memories of my time away and as my Mum actually came with us this ensured our positive adventure.

These accounts note the maturity of the children in accepting their plight: that the expectations they had had of childhood were not to be realised because of war. However, their acceptance did not preclude their understanding that they had been manipulated.

Recollections such as those noted below, illustrate that evacuated children possessed a contemporary awareness of their social status and that, while knowing that they were to be seen and not heard, they were also very insightful and were able to utilise a level of mature discretion even when very young. They understood very well what their situation was and the possibilities thereof not only for their well-being but for a level of exploitation. Betty (from Clydebank) reflects on these difficult times and the social contexts during Britain's war period without actually commenting on the strangeness of being evacuated to a place only a few miles from her home:

> *Anyway my Mum (and I of course) only stayed in Dunoon for a short time when she got a place to rent in Drumchapel a suburb close to Clydebank* [but not that close to the shipyards] *and the house was a miner's row house. But the owner came back within a couple of months and so we got other accommodation in the same area on condition that my mother did the housekeeping. After two years, we got a railway flat. Although most people during this time were very kind, the owner of the railway flat made a lot of money from evacuees: bad to exploit people like this. All that moving must have driven my mother mad – even more so because all the accommodation was almost within walking distance of each other.*

In contemplating their childhoods, the participants indicated a level of realism in their lives as they understood that the dangers of war had rendered them exiles in their own land. As John (from Glasgow) recalled:

> *Yes, I think so* [that the Evacuation was necessary] *because of the threat of the heavy bombing. We used to go to the bottom flat of our building. When we were there the women who lived in that flat*

used to give us tea and things. They were very generous. The houses then had a baffle wall erected in the close. I remember blackout curtains, a pigswill bin how strange and gas mantles. Most people didn't like the idea of the Evacuation but I suppose felt a bit coerced since it was the government who was directing it all and the children knew their place too at least the place that adults had made for us.

Social Change – Contribution of the Evacuation

Fraser's review of the history of social policy credits World War Two with being the harbinger of great social change (1984, pp.241-245), but he also argues that poverty and social deprivation were a result of a rapidly increasing industrialisation highlighting the complexity of increasing demand for appropriate remuneration for labour as well as the booms and slumps in the growth of an industrial economy. Hopkins (1994, pp.318-321) further notes that subsequent to the World War One, the class structure was becoming increasingly anachronistic in the eyes of a population suffering in the face of another war, and exposed to propaganda decrying the injustice of class division. Those interwar years began to witness the emergence of social change.

Social change happened for a variety of reasons after World War Two and this was acknowledged by the participants through their narratives. They alluded regularly to the social conditions prevailing at the time of their Evacuation (in the cities from where many of the participants were evacuated) and compared them with the dramatic changes which had occurred throughout their lives. For example Martin (from Clydebank) remembered:

My friends who were evacuated seemed to accept what had happened but of course these were completely different times. Today we would have had counselling and all that if we had had bad experiences.

Nan, (from Glasgow), in answer to 'how did the host family treat you' replied:

She [only one occupant] was probably indifferent but certainly not unkind. Maybe she needed the money because why else would you have strangers in your house for a whole year? I couldn't imagine doing it myself but different worlds between now and then in the middle of a war of course.

The narrative form, as illustrated in this part of the chapter, confirms the importance of capturing and constructing the participants' Evacuation experiences by contextualising them through their reminiscences from their childhood. The participants' notions of their own childhood evacuation experiences leads to the next part of the chapter which endeavours to define the child in the period leading up to the war and how the child was viewed during the war.

Separation from Family/Significant Others
Of importance to the Scottish Evacuation story is the investigation conducted by Birtchnell and Kennard (1984) which addresses the long term effects on children of separation from caregivers and included former evacuees in their research. Much of the research indicates that **the absence of a mother during the period of the Evacuation era was associated with anxiety and depression in adulthood**. These outcomes are well documented by Barnett (2008) and Altawil (2008). This consciousness of attachment is evidenced by Alec (from Glasgow) in his reply to the question: Did you leave your host family earlier than anticipated?

> *Well, it's hard to be sure about that because I suppose my parents didn't know any better than anyone else about the next step until they were told. What I mean is, there had not been any planning or official bits of paper and the like so my mother probably stayed put until told what was next. But I know that if my mother would have been able to make things better for us by going home at any stage, she would have done that.*

Kathleen (from Dundee), remembering her mother, had this to say:

> *Yes. My Mum, me, and my brother, who was aged 12 and I was aged 14, were evacuated. My Dad was foreman at a jute mill so he didn't come. He was a gentle chap and I remember my Mother was always making strawberry jam and he always gave it away. She was so nice. My Dad was very family minded. I don't reflect that much on it all (evacuation) because it's so long ago, but I cannot imagine at all that it could happen today. Imagine going off to a strange place, strange school and in somebody else's house! Anyway it was OK I think because our mother was there – but still…*

The analyses of Freud, Piaget, and Jung (Hillman in Jenks 1992) who claim that attachment to mother permeates all childhood longings are reflected in the narratives of Alec and Kathryn. With regard to Kathleen's fond memory of her father, as Horn notes the Second World War occurred in a period when fathers began to take a more active role in the upbringing of their children (1989, pp.188-190).

More Leisure

During the pre-war period Scottish city children enjoyed regular Saturday attendance at purpose-built cinemas and many street games, such as chasing and catching games (Mr Wolf, Red Rover, Tig), ball games (Queenie, Keepie-Uppie, Rounders), and indoor games for a dreich[7] day (Stone, Scissors, Paper, Hangman) (Ritchie 1999; Ross 2001).

Although increased leisure was the reality for many city children with the advent of labour saving devices such as washing machines and vacuum cleaners, they still fared less well than their country counterparts. The country children had fields, trees and rivers for adventure and by contrast the city children's playground was often their local streets. Together with the legislation which curtailed child activity in the workforce and the introduction of compulsory education, a further significant change to the life of the Edwardian was that real wages for the working class were successfully negotiated during this period, thereby ensuring that living conditions for many improved dramatically. These changes gave rise to a more gentle and sensitive understanding of the child as a valued member of society (Horn 1989, pp.18-21). It is against this environment of slowly developing change to the view and value of the child that the Evacuation took place.

Evacuee Stereotyping

Although most of the Scottish participants in this study had fond memories of their experiences, it has emerged from studies by Parsons (1999), Holman (1995), and Brown (2000) that many English evacuees experienced troubled recollections, quite the opposite from those smiling excited scrubbed faces, tin cans and labels we have seen in the movies. But the construction of the evacuee did of course change over time.

Typical of the assumptions made by some hosts of their paying guests included:

> The maid was instructed to point out which part of the garden the family could use to remain invisible to their hosts (Longmate 2002, p.58);

and

> In a part of Wigtown, in Scotland, the medical officer, aided by three detachments of V.A.Ds, (Voluntary Aid Detachment) resourcefully bought up all the hair clippers in sight and cut the hair of every mother and child in a particularly verminous detachment of Glaswegians (Longmate 2002, p.52).

Because many of the government evacuees came from the lower socio-economic stratum, the assumption was made perhaps inevitably due to the negative press coverage, that their physical condition would be dirty and verminous among other perorations. This stereotyping is perhaps not surprising given the level of confusion existing in Britain (from the late 1930s) regarding youth and its problems. Indeed from the initial positive depiction, they became inexorably associated with the ascribed behaviours of a less privileged and less well educated class: troublesome and mal-intentioned. However, the narratives of the participants in this study clearly indicate their acceptance that, as child evacuees, their identity had been, to an extent, constructed by the government and assisted by the media of the period. That is, initially the evacuees were sympathetic characters, but over time they became to be regarded as undesirable due to their alleged lack of hygiene and poor manners (Adam 1975, p. 138).

As confirmation of the assumptions made of the working classes, Simmons (2006, p.53) notes that Panter-Downes in her 1971 publication claimed (of 1939) that: 'the war has brought the great unwashed right into the bosoms of the great washed'.

Adherence

The children of the Scottish Evacuation (as well as those from England, Wales and Northern Ireland) of World War II, while remaining peripheral to mainstream politics and policies inasmuch as they had no direct involvement in the decisions of war, were nevertheless directly affected by the government policies generated by war. As John (from Glasgow) asserts in response to the question: 'Did your parents agree with the Evacuation':

> *I don't really know because it was never discussed. But knowing them like I did, I think they would have supported it. They were quite conservative and would have thought it was for our own good. Shame I didn't get round to asking them all the questions you're asking me. Even my Mum didn't criticise anything about our billet, but I suspect there would have been some stuff to criticise. That strikes me as a bit odd because my mother was a very honest char-acter and didn't hide much from us.*

and when asked if the Evacuation was necessary, Isobel (from Glasgow) replied:

> *not necessarily for me; in fact it was a bit of an adventure as it turned out for me. But maybe if I was grown up and had children it would no doubt have been different but we all just did what we were told and we felt important.*

Influence of Authority and 'the Church'

The influence of the established church in Scotland (Church of Scotland: Pres-byterian) was still considerable during the war period, as it had been since the Scottish Reformation in 1560 (Magnusson 2000, p.347). In particular, the church endeavoured to entrench community disapproval of contravention of its teaching on most behaviour, but perhaps concentrating on its notion of 'im-moral behavior'. It is evident that the children of the Evacuation were able to be convinced by adults (as they were convinced by government) to accept the inevitability of war and subsequent Evacuation including the impact upon them. As recalled by Nan (from Glasgow):

> *My mum and dad seemed to support the process initially but thought it was actually a waste of a year in some ways because the situation at the billet was just as bad danger-wise as it would have been at our home. I think I thought that too but I wouldn't have said that out loud to my parents. What I mean is, Scotland not being a very big place, we were never that far away from danger; but of course I might only be thinking that now that I'm talking to*

you about it all. In some ways, because we were churchgoers, I be-
lieve my parents still thought that the advice from the pulpit – no
doubt supporting the 'authority' view of the world – should be ad-
hered to. In general though, I'm not sure how often I have thought
about it over the years. I suspect I haven't even told my children:
how remiss is that?

Nan's response somewhat confirms that she privately questioned the acceptance by her parents of an event which inconvenienced them and which they
concluded was impractical and of no benefit. Nan, however, did not have the
temerity to challenge her parents' authority no matter whence it came, any
more than they were prepared to challenge the authority of the state or the
position of their church.

But it is also obvious from the Scottish participants' clear and perceptive memories that they understood and accepted that they were objects of control. This
is acknowledged by Louise from Glen Luce in the south of Scotland, whose
family billeted several families throughout the Evacuation period:

I think my parents did it (housed evacuees) because they were just
good people who addressed a need at the time. But the evacuees we
sheltered were very well behaved and obedient if you know what I
mean. The Mum helped in the kitchen and the children seemed to
understand that their behaviour was crucial to the success of their
stay. They also very quickly got established in the local church life.
I suspect they would have been churchgoers anyway in their home
town. We all were in those days.

The obedience to authority by both children and adults which prevailed during
this period in Scotland, is a recurring theme in several novels reflective of the
time (Fulton 1999; McArthur and Long 1953; O'Hagan 1999). In these fic-
tional accounts of the 1930s, there are very clear indications that the church
and school were institutions to be respected and obeyed. Obedience was primarily the province of the established church in Scotland from 1560 until the
20th century - Church of Scotland, but due to the influx of Catholics from Ireland during the period 1921-1971 who were attracted to higher wages and the
comfort of the large numbers of Irish migrants already in Scotland, the

Catholic Church gained new prominence and authority. Over time, the Catholic Church's influence sat alongside that of the established church (Mc-Crone 2001, p.13).

A first hand example of the churches' influence is given by Terry (from Clydebank) who pointed out that within the purview of the church, mothers of illegitimate children were met with disapproval. The established church, in its entrenched notion of sexual morality wielded great control in the social life of the population. As Terry mused further on her feelings as a child:

> *According to my mother the Church was an enjoyable part of being away from home and the family was welcomed. Bannockburn is a small town and this [the church] became quite important because she was on her own in a strange place. The church made her feel comfortable. But she apparently was 'watched over' as a single mum. Given that she was so willing to participate in church life and was such a good mum to me, it just doesn't make much sense. As a single mum, she should have been praised for being able to cope on her own. Widows didn't suffer this fate. But that was then and this is now.*

Not everyone yielded to the churches' authority however, and Davies' work (1998, n.p.) draws on research conducted from the late 1800s to 1939 which illustrates how street gangs (predominantly male) which formed in Glasgow during the 1930s, refused to adhere to the strict confines of the church and other dictates. But although unemployment rates ranged in Glasgow between 25 and 33 percent during this period (1930s), none of the established religious organisations at that time contemplated that behaviours were the result of structural forces and poverty.

Surprisingly, none of the Scottish participants alluded to any sectarian relevance in their narratives of their homes or foster homes, at school or among friends, although it was a feature of social divide in Scotland at that time. They all accepted that formal religious adherence was part of their socialisation in their childhoods. As (Kathleen from Dundee) recalled:

> *Yes we went to church, because that's what we did in those days. Everyone went to church in my opinion. I still do, by the way. But the church didn't play any great part in my life as an evacuee we*

85

would have done the same at home. By that, I mean I have become more involved as I got older: I've turned into my mother I think. I suppose we all get a bit pious as we approach you know what.

Win (from Edinburgh) confirmed this:

Of course we went to church while we were away. It was just a part of life then. We were marched to church just as if we were at home.

Marie's (from Glasgow) thoughts suggest some confusion which sometimes assailed the participants in the study as she recalled:

The Minister at our Evacuation place was a bachelor and a bit stodgy. I was a sergeant in the Girls Training Corps so I was pretty involved. In our school playground we mostly were drilled by a big real army sergeant who shouted all the time. We were quite proficient and could about turn and march quite smartly. Our purpose was to be able to carry messages by bicycle and generally be useful in the event of an invasion. We must have been recruited by the Church I think. I can still remember the wee song. Now that I think about it, what propaganda.

> *We're here to help our country*
> *Shoulder her heavy load*
> *This is the way to victory*
> *This is the surest road.*
> *CHORUS*
> *We are cadets of the GTC*
> *Our youth to our country we bring*
> *Willing and ready we'll always be*
> *To serve our God and our King.*
> *Firm and united we shall stand*
> *Whatever may come our way*
> *Striving to help our native land*
> *Soon may she win the day.*

Social Progress and Enlightenment

Social commentators such as Sir Thomas Lipton, The Guild of Aid, and Dr Nora Wattie, who was principal officer of Health for Maternity and Child Welfare in Glasgow and who achieved international recognition for her work (cited in King 1993), advanced the notion that the delinquency problem was related to the breakdown of family and the later displacement caused by conditions of war; but there existed some ambivalence regarding the social behaviour during the 1930s, which illustrates the complexities resulting from times of great social unrest Smith (2007, pp.78-105).

Interestingly, rather than imposing an authoritarian solution, those in charge at the time (in Scotland) adopted a benign approach endeavouring to institute social solutions of a reformist nature rather than of a punishment regimen. Ultimately it was concluded that, not surprisingly, juvenile delinquency was the result of poor housing, lack of leisure facilities and underemployment and would need to be addressed socially. This welfarist approach reflected the Fabian spirit of the time (Davies 1998 n.p.).

One of the outcomes of these reformist endeavours was the establishment of service organisations such as for the girls, the Girls Training Corps and for the boys, the Air Training Corps. Children and young adults in Scotland during the period of Evacuation lived then in mixed realities: one of rebellion and indiscipline and the other of adherence to the moral dictates of the established churches and educational establishments. This ambivalence was exacerbated by the poor socio-economic situation of some of the children and youth.

Nevertheless in the 1930s, the period of the lead up to the Evacuation, children's lives were still largely governed by economics, as Kynaston notes (2007, pp. 20-21):

> As early as January 1941, while the bombs were falling, *Picture Post* outlined in a celebrated special (complete with six naked, presumably impoverished small children on the cover 'A Plan for Britain' ... drawn up by the eminent economist and civil servant ... set out proposals for a comprehensive post-war system of social security ... a classic welfare state ...

and as Fraser (1984, p.214) reported the ideas of Seebohm Rowntree:

> I think it is probable that after the war a scheme of family al-
> lowances will be introduced and national minimum wages
> will be fixed and I think it is almost certain that the scale of
> benefits under the various social insurance schemes will be
> raised to levels which will provide the families concerned
> with the essentials of physical efficiency. I think therefore
> that there is no need to be seriously concerned about the con-
> tinuation of extreme poverty (Seebohm Rowntree).

But to generalize across Britain in 1939 is to over-simplify the social cleavages. Furthermore, it is acknowledged that perceptions of the value of children in 1939 were not necessarily shared across the United Kingdom. For example, the situation in Scotland, during World War II, when juvenile delinquency emerged as a serious issue of law and order, the Scottish Office established a Child Saving movement. This movement had at its core the belief that the lawlessness was the result of, among other justifications, the father's absence due to military service. The Child Saving Movement discouraged the use of corporal punishment for delinquent acts which was not the prevailing strategy in Scotland at that time to address lawlessness. Probation became the preferred option. That in Scotland, child and young adult crime and punishment re-ceived such comprehensive attention illustrates the leap which was taken in the middle of the 20th century regarding the value of the child. The child had indeed become the person (Smith 2007, pp.78-105).

It is somewhat surprising that in all of the social debates during the war period, there is no mention of the behaviours of the children who were evacuated in their thousands except as recorded by the local media.

British Life during World War II –
What about the children, including the Evacuees?

Many accounts, both fiction and non-fiction have been written of British life during the war years, and most were concerned with the life of adults. For ex-ample, an anthology of women's writing (edited by Hartley 1994) during the period, offers a wonderful collection of stories from women ranging from factory workers to fashion editors. These include their more mundane struggles to find provisions such as an onion or some carrots. Although life was very difficult for most, there also existed the much lauded stoicism and humour represented by the cartoon industry, which often made light of a dire situation (Briggs 1975, p.75; p.94).

But there were few stories about children and the level of austerity to which they were exposed and no acknowledgement that life for children was just as complex as that of adults during World War Two. This complexity is highlighted and outlined by Childs (1995, pp.62-63) who in endeavouring to condense this complexity, notes the influences of war on the adult population who **did not** go to war and on **those who served in the forces**. Childs acknowledges that those who served in the war had endured unimaginable horror while also acknowledging that the implications of the war also had great bearing on the lives of the home population which, of course, included the children, but the lives of children were rarely examined.

Conclusion

It is a given that children have often been the innocent victims of war perpetrated by adults. The suffering of children during and after World War One resulted in the establishment of the Save the Children Fund in 1919 (Palmer 1997, p.7). This was followed in 1924, by the Declaration of the Rights of the Child (commonly known as the 'Declaration of Geneva') promulgated by the League of Nations. The rights of the children of the Evacuation therefore fell under the Declaration during the Evacuation process. However, the Declaration, the only legislation enacted relative to the rights of children applicable to Britain in 1939, is silent on the issue of separation of children from their parents. Therefore any obligation on the government to comply with specific legislation regarding children was ill-defined, at best.

Three central issues have emerged from this chapter on the understanding of the construction and sociology of the British child of the Evacuation period. These issues have emerged primarily through the narratives of the participants. The first is that socio-economic conditions - in Scotland their level of religious adherence and obligation to authority - largely defined the domestic life of the children. Secondly, children are always vulnerable in the adult world and thirdly, children are more easily manipulated than adults, although they often understand the requirement for and benefit of acquiescence. Children must therefore be afforded the same respect as that offered to adults, because we must not assume that we know the thoughts of a child.

CHAPTER SEVEN:

MEMORY, HISTORY AND REMEMBRANCE

Writing of course deepens the moveable theme of memory a writ-
ten-down memory is not exactly the same as what was remembered,
and memories change and reorder themselves over time … What we
now know about memory, is that writing things down, taking notes,
is also a form of not remembering. The brain surrenders memories
remembered by the hand; so the act of writing offers a counterpoint
to memory as well as an account of it (Richards 2009, p.190)

Introduction

Memory is a complex concept because there are numerous variables. They come in the shape of rote memory such as songs, poetry, times tables, and intangibles such as pictures, gardens, buildings, books and clothing. However, this chapter is concerned with cognitive memory, which is related to the evacuees' recall of their experiences, notwithstanding the assistance provided by the intangibles noted above. Although the current literature maintains the notion of a 'collective memory' this chapter argues against this suggesting that all memory is specific to the individual and cannot be replicated by others' notions of events.

Theories of memory include, among others, individual, collective, constructed, history, public, revisionist, national, and international. Memory theories are enhanced by those of remembrance and commemoration which are symbolic and cultural and are immortalised in heritage, built fabric such as museums, installations such as exhibitions and in music, film, and literature. All of these concepts emerge in the narratives of the participants and all are related to the period of their Evacuation as well as to the overarching context of wartime. The memories of the participants have also supplemented the recording of the formal history of the World War Two period, the public memory of which was remarkably still evoked in 2009. This is evidenced by the many commemorative events held during 2009, such as those held by the Russian and Bulgarian Leaders in Gdansk (*The Sofia Echo* 2009), the USA Holocaust Museum in Washington: Embassy of the Republic of Poland (www.washington. polemb.net), Embassy of the Republic of Poland, and the Republic of the Philippines, Department of Foreign Affairs (dfa.gov.ph/).

Since this chapter is principally about the application of the various memory theories, the following narratives' illustrate the power and legitimacy of the personal memory and of course are the whole point of this story/book.

According to Betty (from Clydebank):

> *We stayed in the gym for four months then to a house in Alexandria which is town near Clydebank but about 12 miles away. It was necessary to stagger school hours and teachers because many had been evacuated. We stayed in the house in Alexandria for a further four months and then we stayed in another house in Renton (about ten miles from Clydebank) for a further four months. Some people seem to remember a very organized event, but my recall is that we got instructions by word of mouth.*

Walter (from Clydebank), however, remembered other aspects of the same events:

> *We were told by megaphone to go to the local school from where we were to be 'despatched' to various places. We were not allowed to go back to the flat. In due course three buses came along to take us to our billets and as we moved out in a convoy, the buses were strafed. Initially the family were to a local school - Renton Primary - and we were 'housed' in the gym with many other evacuees.*

Betty's and Walter's memories of the same event illustrate well that their recollections are unique to them. The evacuees not only had their personal
memories, they were also, although subliminally given their age, subjected
to the public representation of wartime. That is, the political and media representation of the war generated the subsequent public memory. Both were
constructed by the government and were subsumed into the individual consciousness and memories of the population. In order to promote the policy
of Evacuation, parents and children had to be convinced that it was incum-
bent upon them to comply with the decision to evacuate millions of people
from their homes.

As Douglas, a Londoner, remembered:

> *When we arrived from the train we were taken to this big hall
> where for some reason we all marched in a circle and people looked
> us up and down. I wasn't scared or anything but when I think of it
> now with the knowledge of the death camps, it was a really strange
> thing to make us do. As it turned out, I had really nice people to
> stay with Burnley in Lancashire. We all made fun of each other's
> accents. I think I am lucky that I have the disposition I have because
> when I have discussed this with anyone else (which is not very often
> by the way), their eyes fill up because they think it was awful to be
> lined up to be picked when I wasn't sure what I was being picked
> for. I think it was all a bit of an adventure for me.*

All the participants were aware of the possibility that the longer one is removed
from the event, the more the prospect of inaccurate reconstruction increases,
as does the interplay with imagination. Jenny (from Clydebank) told me:

> *Well, I have thought a bit about it over the years, but funnily enough
> I've thought about it more recently and I don't know why - just get-
> ting old I suppose and scared it will get less clear. There's been a bit
> about it all in the papers over the last couple of years and then you
> turned up, funny that. It was all a bit strange. I wonder what would
> happen today. I wouldn't think I would want to stay with strangers
> - maybe I would have stayed at home given the chance.*

The foregoing indicates that the memories of the participants' accounts of their Evacuation, including references to the war, were both intensely personal and perceptively social in context.

Is not all memory personal and individual?

Given that evacuees' memories were cognitively theirs, it is argued that the concept of collective memory (currently an academic focus) cannot be a legitimate reflection of events. However, that accounts of social events can be constructed within a group, due to monuments, plaques, street names - the most significant of these being the official declaration and conclusion of the war - then the notion of a collective *account* in these circumstances can run in parallel with personal memory. An example of the personal *detailed* memory of the events of the evacuees' upheaval by Betty (from Clydebank) as forthcoming:

> *What happened was that on the night of 13/14 March 1941, the sirens went off in Clydebank and all hell broke loose. We were aware that massive bombing was taking place and we were all terrified. We didn't even have any shelters at that time. The whole family which was my Mum and Dad [myself] and my two younger sisters, plus lots of others in our close, went to the doctor's place across the street because he had a basement. He let us all stay the night there which I suppose was quite kind of him. The next morning my Mum and my two sisters and I got up and managed to get a taxi and got on a ferry which was going from Gourock to Dunoon, our Evacuation location.*

This experience is mutually exclusive and of course personal. That is, as noted previously, all the participants' memories are relative to their particular family and extended family; the social and personal. Indeed, it is argued that all memory must, by definition, be social and personal because we are all unique beings. Chris (from Dundee) articulated this very clearly when he said:

> *Well, I still have great memories about it [the Evacuation] and still think about it a lot. Now that I think about it I did go looking for the house in Banchory because it had an anvil under the house but I didn't ever find it. I really appreciated how kind the family*

were to us. Can't believe I remember the anvil story: what on earth was that about (smiles).

John's social and personal recollection was also evident as he reflected on the paradoxical situation in which he, and others, found themselves as evacuees:

I went on to live the rest of my life in Glasgow and didn't see any bombs, but I knew about Clydebank but we were in Ayrshire at the time, and I suppose we missed that. One thing though was that although we were in the war, it was like we weren't part of it. When we came back it was like it had all happened somewhere else.

The theorists' contributions to the memory debates have had some significance for this work.

However, the evacuees' perceptions of events and their interpretation are an individual memory and cannot become part of the collective since the perceptions are unique to the person. Therefore social and individual memory is concerned often with the mundane wisps of individual life but the notion of a collective memory must have at its core an event which can be recalled exactly by more than one individual. That is, social memory is related to the history but does cannot become a *collective memory*: perhaps a collective *remembrance* is legitimate since all of us can read of an event which can be corroborated, but it is not a collective *memory*.

To further confirm the personal memory, there are many, diverse and varied accounts of the participants in this research in response to the same questions are remarkable; for example, Ken (from Dagenham) stated in answer to the question: How were you informed about the Evacuation process?

Not sure why but my aunties and uncles told us all about it and they always said things like, 'How come it's good enough for the King not to send his children away'. Anyway one of the aunties with her husband took me to their place where there was a railway at the back. I often went to pick up coal to keep the home fires burning. So I was essentially not a government evacuee. I suppose I must have gone to rural Essex, but I don't remember anything official – of course I was only 8 –I guess I just trusted anyone in the family.

Similarly, Isobel (from Glasgow) said:

I think I just heard from local talk but the school seemed to be the place to get the information. Although my Evacuation was a private one, lots of school children from Glasgow ended up in Biggar so we must have found out from school in the first place I suppose. It's silly, but I don't remember ever even asking that question. It is probably quite significant to your work though – you know, research.

By contrast Robert (from Glasgow) related that:

I presume through the school but there was so much activity and gossip around the hotel where my father worked about the war in general and we were privy to a lot of that. Surely we must have been told in some official capacity, but I honestly can't remember that. I just remember it all seemed to happen quite quickly and we were off.

Nancy (from Glasgow) also recalled:

Well because there was no warning about the Blitz, I presume it was just word of mouth. I just remember being 'organised' so I suppose my mother and father must have been given some instructions. Must have been word of mouth to me, I think. Imagine I've never found that out: now I'm really curious so I will now check it all out.

Because they were so young at the time of their Evacuation, and that they shared a similar environment, it is probable that the sources of their Evacuation were also similar such as family, friends, school, parents, workplaces etc. Nevertheless their responses differed from each other and again confirmation that that all memory is social and personal.

James (from Glasgow) recalls:

> *I think we got notices from school and we were told where to as-*
> *semble and what to bring and then we got the gasmasks when we*
> *were getting on the train. I don't remember thinking much of it*
> *really. My mother must have understood what it was about and*
> *just gave us our orders.*

Gordon, (also from Glasgow), recalled that:

> *Our school gave us bits of paper to take home to our parents. Also,*
> *it was all over the place on the radio and posters and everybody was*
> *talking about what was going to happen to us children. To be honest*
> *though I couldn't get enough of it because I was quite excited I have*
> *to say. I suppose on reflection my parents wouldn't have been think-*
> *ing that way though, would they? All very well with hindsight.*

Therefore, although official propaganda denigrated non official communication as a dangerous practice, the government depended upon information
being spread by word of mouth as well as by more formal means. In fact, as
pointed out by several evacuees, it was not only a useful conduit it was also,
for them, a credible one.

Physical Outcomes of Memory

How bodies remember is the topic of Kleinman and Kleinman's 1994 work
particularly related to the experiences in the aftermath of China's Cultural
Revolution: 1969 1976 (in Schoenhals 2005, p.277) Their theory is based on
the question: How does the societal disorientation caused by a crisis such as
the Chinese Cultural Revolution manifest itself in a physical sense? For some,
the memory of the historical experience of the revolution was manifested in
dizziness, exhaustion and pain. The Kleinmans suggest that these physical effects were the result of the merging of the social and physical body pain.

A memory, especially a particularly significant or traumatic memory, in some
cases is accompanied by a physical sensation, such as pain. As Irene (originally
from Bristol) recounted, some evacuees' war experience memories especially
when associated with trauma, also included the physical.

On the 7ᵗʰ December 1941 when I got to school in Hong Kong on the lunch break we heard aeroplanes and they were from Japan. We were herded into the class rooms and we stayed in them for three days. Two nuns eventually escorted me home to my Mum at the flat. We were taken to Stanley Fort: my Mum and Dad and three servants and my brother and sister. At the fort the conditions were extremely primitive. We spent Boxing Day there and then we went back home because my Mum presumed the war had been won by the British. But on the way back to our own flat, we had to pass these Japanese soldiers and the children were lined up and humiliated by them. Mum was taken by the soldiers, and we children went over to assist her. I can remember there was a pit in the room where we were taken and just as we all thought we were about to be executed, some Japanese soldiers who had been educated in America rescued us. After the ordeal, we did see many atrocities. The pain of those atrocities is still with me. Sometimes I get a knot in my stomach when I remember the horror when my Mum was grabbed by the soldiers: I thought we were going to die. Not so much now but for a long time it was physical pain I felt every time I saw a uniform which didn't have to be Japanese of course. I clearly remember a runner who came and gave us news that we had surrendered to the Japanese on Boxing Day 1941.

As noted above, Irene did acknowledge some ongoing physical pain associated with her memory of her experience in Hong Kong which is not surprising given she experienced some physical as well as cognitive discomfort at best and trauma at worst.

Irene's experience confirms that memory bears more that only the cognitive effects and can also be manifested in physical outcomes. An experience such as Irene's within which she remembers via her body experience, is profound. To re-imagine a situation where she might have witnessed her mother's murder causes ongoing pain. Irene's story is different from those of all the other participants because she was an evacuee who was a part of the war. By contract, the others reminisced often in their narratives that although they felt they were in the war, no-one seemed to understand this at the time or when they went home.

Intended forgetting

To have the ability to choose to forget negative experiences would be beneficial to recovery from them. However, a study undertaken by Lee *et al.* (2007) indicates that intended forgetting is difficult to achieve. That is, to endeavour to continually ignore or suppress the information which the individual wishes to forget is not an effective way to forget. Indeed Lee's findings corroborated those of others in the field inasmuch as the only effective means of suppression is to substitute other information in order to inhibit the target information. Although the position of Lee *et al.* is supported by Payne and Corrigan (2007), they add further and important results to the theory: that people can often intentionally forget mundane events; however directed forgetting does not appear to apply to emotional events. Can intended forgetting therefore be achieved?

Desai (2006, pp.142-143) wrote in her account of a shared historical legacy and a common experience of impotence and humiliation:

> He had lived with Gyan's family until he died, but they never discovered where he travelled to or which countries he had fought against. He came of a generation, all over the world for whom it was easier to forget than to remember and the more their children pressed, the more their memory dissipated.

Like this character, some participants had not before discussed the own experiences and although social exclusion was not a major issue for most of the participants, Barbara from London referred to her experience:

> *However, I do feel quite sad, almost a physical sensation when I reflect on it all. It bothers me so much that neither of my parents felt the need to come to visit in all that time. This is a long time we are talking about in the life of a young girl like me. I am still troubled by this but was never able to raise it because I was scared of the possible outcome. Maybe I thought they would say they didn't miss me.*

Win (from Edinburgh) remembered:

> *Yes, I was homesick for most of the time and also I was sad because my Dad had just died. We were not a big extended family so my*

siblings – who were older and did not accompany and mother and me were the biggest part of my life. Sometimes the longing was almost physical.

Marie (from Clydebank) said:

I didn't feel isolated in a general sense because I was used to moving about a bit to relatives in the country before the war and anyway my mother was with me. But I felt a bit isolated from my father and from his life which had involved me quite a bit since he was a General Practitioner. I longed to have that experience back again and since it still makes me a bit sad I wish I could forget that longing because there is no logic to holding on to it – it's all gone.

Although few of the participants exhibited the social exclusion noted above in Barbara's text, there is much anecdotal evidence in the stories of evacuees already published, in which the pain of social exclusion did in fact translate to physical pain. However, more recently, Heinl's (2006, pp.61-65) work offers several examples of his success with an 'intuitive approach' to discovery and exploration of childhood war trauma. In this paper, he offers powerful examples of his case studies which illustrate the long-term psychological damage caused by child war trauma, explaining his use of intuition, resulting from a level of self-observation. Doogue (2011, p.13), on the anniversary of Victory in the Pacific Day on August 15, reflects on how it would be for thousands of Australians and will be 'full of memories'. She also notes as in the words of one veteran years after his time at war: 'on our return home, we were told not to talk about our experiences. We were profoundly changed men but received no assistance to deal with the psychological and sometimes physical needs'. As well, the article notes even this far away from the events of war, 'people become physically disabled ... because they have time to think, reflect on their lives'.

The memories of the participants in this book fall between the historical and social since the historical events and policies of the time created and concluded their memories. But whether or not the participants were influenced by written records, newsreels, or re-construction via media, their perspectives of their experiences belong only to them.

It could be argued that intended forgetting is the antithesis of nostalgia even when incredibly; nostalgia is induced when remembering the regimen of Joseph Stalin[8], from 1922 until his death in 1953. As Kirkwood (2009, n.p.) notes, Stalin was voted third greatest Russian ever in a nationwide TV poll in 2008 in Russia on the basis of nostalgia for a time when life was much better and easier [under Stalin]:

> there was always bread in the shops. This phenomenon illustrates a level of intended forgetting that life under Stalin was brutal and repressive for most even after the war years. It is therefore argued that intended forgetting can be a tool of survival from trauma.

Several evacuees exhibited a desire to achieve an intended forgetting, because when engaged in discourse during the interview process, they suggested that they could not answer some sections of the questionnaire due to their lack of recall and some suggested that perhaps they had consciously forgotten. As Douglas (from London) claimed at the beginning of the interview:

> *You can ask all the questions you like, but I can't remember a bloody thing; OK off you go and interrogate me but I'm not sure I can help you – but we'll see.*

However, his initial reluctance does not necessarily suggest that that he was intending to forget any more than other participants' initial reluctance to tell their story. It may or may not be evidence of an intention to deliberately forget. In fact, Douglas in due course had a recall as particular as the other participants. Perhaps they were simply unsure that their story had any relevance for the book.

Although the evaluation of the participants' narratives was that most found it easy to remember their experiences and their reactions to them, there is a body of literature which suggests that it is possible to construct positive retrospective evaluations of prominent events in life although these events possessed negative elements. Although Agnes (from Glasgow) indicated in her narrative that her overall Evacuation experience was:

a very positive experience because I became independent at a very young age, camaraderie, a bit of discipline I might not have had in the city, I had lots of freedom in the country, it was very safe in the country ... and I think I benefitted greatly from the experience. Of course my own children and grandchildren have been reared very well in the city; so now it all sounds a bit precious...

she also recalled

but I was homesick all the time and even though my mother was there, I never did get back to Glasgow in the three years I was away so that made me sad as well as being able to enjoy the Evacuation experience. I sort of choose to forget the sad bit.

Agnes's ambivalence illustrates that her experiences were tinged with some negative elements. Nevertheless, this was not the case with the majority of the Scottish evacuees interviewed.

As Kathleen (from Dundee) confirmed:

I have fond memories about the lovely countryside and the independence we enjoyed. Our place was on the edge of a village. I do remember how much I fancied one of the boys at the house in Banchory, but I don't suppose he fancied me back because I was a lot poorer than he was and I was always worried about how to use the cutlery and things. I do reminisce a bit from time to time.

and as Nancy recalled:

I remained at Corry for about 18 months and remember it as 'idyllic'. I felt secure and loved there and don't remember a single harsh word, although I was never a little angel. The maid was also just one of the household. Haymaking was great fun for a little girl, and I know that they also grew corn, potatoes and turnip: no turnip has ever tasted as good as the little ones I regularly pulled from the field, peeled and washed in the burn (stream).

*The farm house was adequate but washing in my case was rudi-
mentary because there was never any water in the bathroom! There
was a huge oak tree which was just visible high above the road on
the last bend before the keeper's cottage. I was told I mustn't go up
to it but given no further explanation. None was needed. You don't
take chances with a ghost. My brother told me that the version he
was told was that the oak tree was used as gallows to hang local vil-
lains. Please bear in mind that these are the recollections of a young
girl written over 60 years after the event. Time may well have
blurred the edges or added rose-coloured tinges to my memories and
might also have obliterated unpleasant ones. But what you have
here are my recollections however faulty of a very happy time in an
idyllic location.*

Memory and History

Social memory and its relationship to the construction of formal history is an
exciting contemplation, particularly as one understands the level of its importance and usefulness. But social historians do not necessarily claim to seek the
truth, rather they seek truth in their pursuit of accuracy. Memory is rather
about a cognitive experience which might or might not be true to the political
history. The political history of this work is that of evacuees' memories of
World War Two in the social context of the time spent away from the theatre
of war as well as from extended family and friends. These are the memories of
children whose experiences of that time are fashioned by their knowledge of
a war which, although real, was rather unreal to them. The social memories
of several of the participants were of being exiled in their own country during
a great international conflict, and they understood that active participation in
the war was quite distinct from the circumstances of the evacuated children.
Only recently has the social importance of the evacuee experiences and memories come to light and their importance to the official history of World War
Two. Cathie (from Clydebank) explained:

*What I mean is because we were I suppose in some ways isolated
from it, it was presumed that we didn't have to worry about it. But
of course we all had families who were away from home and fight-
ing and all that. So although we were not really 'in it', we were
affected by it.*

In centring her discussion of memory and children as they relate to the history of World War Two, Krips (2000, p.6) suggests that children's memories are 'those of children imagined by adults on behalf of children'. The memories of the evacuees during World War Two have a relationship, albeit not a profound one, to the literature of the period. Jack when rejecting the classics of the time in favour of the comics, the *Beano* and the *Dandy*, indicated that for him the comics were an essential component of *his* Evacuation memory. As Jack recalls in answer to a question about school in his Evacuation location:

> *It was fine and I don't remember any drama, but I think it was easy because of the comfort of having mum with me. Although it was a very small school we were exposed to lots of what we would now call Classics of their time like 'The railway children' 'The water babies' but also just the right time for the Beano and the Dandy' and yes, before you ask me, they were all for boys. By the way I never ever understood Alice in Wonderland or the other one he [Lewis Carroll] wrote. I've never lifted them again and didn't encourage my children to read them. Now, the Beano and the Dandy and Hotspur, these were quite a different kettle of fish!'*

His enjoyment of the comics is no less important for the historical construction of his experience than if he had read those books he called the Classics. In fact, the possibility exists that the comics might well have represented the times more accurately than the literature of that time because they were contemporary accounts of Jack's life. Naturally, the familiarity of comics might have alleviated some of the children's strange (to them) circumstances and situations. The representativeness and importance of the comics to the evacuees' memory, is confirmed by Samuel (1994). Samuel is a social historian, a contributor to the journal *Past and Present*, who has developed a hybrid approach to memory using the tools of cultural theory as much as social history inasmuch as he utilises as many 'things' as he does recorded human reflections. These include books and photographs and in particular retro-chic objects and fashion.

Memory's assistance with history is highlighted by as Betty (from Clydebank) recalled:

> *A few years ago for some reason I was part of something for the Clydebank Press but it wasn't much. I've talked a lot more to you and I've enjoyed it. Will you come back? All those memories, so clear after all. My family had all intended to go to New Zealand before the war but I was diagnosed with polio when I was one year old so that was the end of New Zealand. I had to wait until I was 18 before I got surgery and all my bones were broken to fix me and I survived. How different things would have been if I had not had polio. But that's history for you.*

This nexus between memory and history is well articulated by Barbara, a Londoner, who described her Evacuation experience:

> *I was away for over three years. While we were away, we didn't really know that much about what was going on in the war. Officially, I mean. It was like we were apart from it all, and yet over the years when I have watched movies or newsreels or read books and all that, it seems strange that all that was going on when I was living away from it all. It was like we had to learn about what life in England was like when we were actually there – well Wales, but you know what I mean. All those battles and all those soldiers roaming around the place and we were nowhere near the action as it were. Imagine having to read about what happened while you were in your own country. We hardly knew a thing.*

Barbara was able to discern that *her* memory of the war years was that it had never been properly reflected in the history books. That is, to Barbara, the war years were those of exclusion and quite unrelated in some ways to the importance of the monumental events of World War Two. The official history did not really touch or represent her.

Whilst Klein's position (2000) is that memory and history are mutually exclusive, Young (1993) makes memory, although not quite a hero, an active agent in the construction of history. How else can history be developed if not from the experiences of those who were 'in it'. Jim's (from Clydebank) response in answer to whether the hosts were kind to them is a very important element of the history of Rennie Macintosh's architectural iconic building: Hillhouse in Helensburgh in Scotland:

> *They were very kind and actually let us get on with things without a great deal of interference. There seemed to be some negotiation however regarding domestic roles, for example, cooking. This would have been occasioned by Mother wishing to cook for her own family. This negotiation took place between Mother and the servants not between my mother and the owners. Who would not be happy in a situation where a large family had moved only a few miles away from a very crowded small flat to the most amazing example of the zenith of Scottish art and architecture: the Rennie Macintosh 'Hill House' with many rooms, huge grounds and even a school room! Imagine having five servants upstairs. Oh happy days. But I understand that to live with strangers in a war situation when everyone was so scared etc was not my wonderful experience but mine still deserves its place in the overall history of the evacuation. It's my story and I've often told it, but how great would it be to be published with all the other stories you have already.*

As evidenced by this chapter, the twin scholarly pursuits of memory and history have been at times deconstructed by the academy, but to what end? Memory, no matter how it is labelled, is one of the most significant contributors to the production of history, and without the record of the memories of those who have experienced 'history', history itself must be incomplete.

Through this diary, the Scottish Evacuation participants have now played their part in the construction of the history of World War Two as it relates to the Scottish as well as the British evacuation experiences. The memories of the evacuees sit alongside and contribute to the recorded history of the great social changes which took place during and after the war. These are their role in history as Jim further claimed in answer to the question: Have you ever discussed your experience in detail before?

Yes, for the National Trust. I told my story to them for a special project being undertaken about five years ago. But that story was really more about my war experience. What I mean is that my story was concerned with how I felt about the war, not about my Evacuation experience. It was a start but I had hoped that the Evacuation experience would have been just as important, if not more important to an historian or a project such as the National Trust one because of course the Evacuation was a very big part of the war, at least in my terms and in Scottish terms or British for that matter. The fact that a poor family like ours ended up living in such luxury was an important outcome of an unintended social experiment and I think it was a very interesting outcome and should have had its place in the whole war story. Anyway I've told you now so you can put it in your book so that at least some people will understand that we really were a very important component of the British history of the World War Two.

Before closing the chapter the following excerpts from the evacuees' stories confirm memory's important relationship to formal history:

A conundrum from Louise who was not an evacuee but whose family hosted several families, not just evacuees, during the war is that:

A local couple, the Withers, who were big landowners, offered to look after a Prisoner of War, William, who was with the family for the duration of the war. William ended up staying with the family and became 'Scottish'. He was also a friend of Allan, my brother, who remembers that William said of the Withers family, 'They treated me like a son'.

As Harry (from Croydon) recalled:

We were evacuated to Norwich in Norfolk by train and when we got there we were taken to a big hall where we were interviewed. We were taken around Norwich where the case officer knocked on doors to see if anyone would take us in. We did get a place and stayed there for about six weeks with a woman who was on her own. But my mother caught her using our ration cards for her own use so that was the end of her. The billeting people were really nice and managed to get us a cottage which had two rooms which had to double as bedrooms, lounge and kitchen. It was really old but did have running water and an outside toilet. We really quite liked it as Mum used to bake bread in this big oven. This cottage was situated in the grounds of a monastery so we had loads to explore and play in. My twin sister was often found sitting in the cloisters singing and talking to the monks. There were lots of American servicemen around at the time and we used to say 'Any gum chum' and they would give us chewing gum or chocolate. They used to put on parties for us evacuees and we got lots of stuff we wouldn't otherwise have got during the war. It's a good story isn't it?

Conclusion

The relevance of the theories of remembering and forgetting cannot be over emphasised. In particular the intersections across the memory literature genre have grounded and enabled understanding of the participants' narratives as they relate to their recall of their experiences which were often rather complex and mature. The concepts of the field of memory inquiry as they relate to the development of history have also been interrogated in this chapter. The relationship between memory and history and the current broad debate relative to the notions of the individual and collective memory have been especially challenging.

CHAPTER EIGHT:

WE COPED RATHER WELL, THANK YOU

Autobiography exposes 'the worst deceiver of all   we make up our pasts' (Lessing in McKenna 2007)

This chapter examines and discusses the reflections and findings of the participants relative to their time spent in country locations. Many evacuees had embraced their time in the country, maintaining that they had benefited in some way while away from their homes in the major urban centres of Scotland or England. According to the narratives of the Scottish evacuees, these positive outcomes were not concerned necessarily with the accommodation or other physical conditions which were in many cases of a considerably higher standard than those of their homes in the city. In fact, their positive experiences emanated mainly from their proximity to the countryside as a counterpoint to their lives in the city. For many of the Scottish evacuees, their Evacuation was not significantly distanced from their own homes.

But, for many of the English evacuees, the distances (given the period of their Evacuation) was much further from home, which resulted in the inability of their parents to easily visit the unaccompanied children.

The chapter investigates other issues such as Social Self-awareness, Nostalgia, and Resilience.

But we thought we were just the same as Everybody Else
Through their narratives, the Scottish participants indicated that they saw themselves as 'ordinary', but certainly not underprivileged.

Most of the evacuees were very young at the time of their exile, but their thoughts (retrospectively) on their experiences substantially contradict the stereotypical views of child evacuees – unclean, ill-mannered and lacking in education. In the first instance, the participants in had no particular notion of their relative social privation and when interviewed them in 2007, 2008 and 2009, they were interested only minimally in the perceptions of them by the social and political historians.

They insisted that they were well looked after and nurtured by their families, had respect for others and had good standards of hygiene: indeed the opposite to their portrayal by the media and the middle classes of the time. They did, however mostly live in rented tenement flats which afforded little privacy and had limited space. But because that was the world they knew, that of the world of their families, friends and school friends who found themselves in similar situations - the evacuees made little of their home social conditions. However, as James points out when comparing his lifestyle in Glasgow with that of his billet:

> *It was a wonderful big house with a putting green. The house had 15 rooms and was in Lenzie which is about 60 miles from Glasgow. It all came to an end though because I contracted a very bad poisoning in my leg which kept me from school for nine months and had to back to the city. The old woman who owned the place loved me so much she wanted to adopt me. She bought my brother and me a tandem and we used it all through the war. The memory of this house is so clear. Can you imagine the size of this place? I have never seen anything like it since: even in my comfortable life after the War. I can just imagine how my mother felt when the owner wanted to adopt me. I never did find out if she wanted to adopt my brother too. We laughed about that for a long time throughout our lives when we shared a beer: or two!*

While the Scottish evacuees of this study did not see themselves as they were allegedly anticipated by many of their host families, the perception persisted and appeared to be readily accepted by the other classes: so much so that the host families and the local organizations felt obliged to undertake a civilizing mission to 'make decent citizens of 95% of them' (*Aberdeen University Review* 1940). This journal article discussed a strand of middle-class Scottish opinion, in relation to the Scottish evacuees, which was skeptical about the urban working class, especially those of Irish Catholic origin. The perception of the middle-class was that the evacuees would have two main characteristics: they were 'inured to dependent pauperism ... self-help and independence seems unknown; and they regularly made "false statements"'.

Although this article notes the incidence of both religious and ethnic prejudice and the impact of 'cheap strike-breaking Irish' on 'Scotland's industrial heartland' this is somewhat surprising because, as Stewart and Welshman point out (2006, p.113), reference to sectarianism was rarely raised in the public domain in that period, particularly in a publication from an eminent university such as Aberdeen.

The popular press at the time also had their notion of the poor state of the evacuees in general. For example *The News Chronicle* (October 1939, cited in Crosby, 1986, pp.44-45) stated that:

> householders were not prepared to receive into their decent homes filthy children whose personal hygiene is worse than those of some domestic animals and 'if the millions spent on much-boosted social services in London should not produce better results than these'.

Similarly, the *Glasgow Herald* (1939, 21 September p.8) reported:

> that the Evacuation of Glasgow children to Dumfriesshire had led to problems, with the local Education Committee claiming that a third of the children examined had to be excluded from school because of the presence of lice or disease. Some householders were refusing to take evacuees, and the 'difficulty is increased by presence in the district of a large number of mothers with young children over whom the Education Committee have no control'.

The above newspaper articles indicate again that while the Scottish and other British Evacuations had distinct differences, unfortunately the negative stereotyping was one of the stronger impressionistic views which prevailed in all cases.

In support of the civilising mission, there were many country residents who, as noted in the article, on reviewing the situation of the evacuees several months into their stay in the country, declared:

> What a handsome testimonial to our working-class house-holders, and what an object lesson on the value of upbringing and environment … and the long and particularly Scottish practice of seeking to "save" pauper children by removing them from urban slums and placing them in what was thought to be a regenerative rural environment (MacDonald 2006, p.2).

Such was the impression of one rural middle class individual relative to her city cousins, but it is one that is not consonant with those of most of the Scottish participants. As Nan (from the west end of Glasgow) recalled:

> *The house had only a single woman in it a bit odd when I think about it. My Mum, Dad and I lived in one room which had cooking facilities. My Mum stayed at home with me and Dad used to check on our own house as often as possible. At one time the windows of our flat in the inner city were blown in due to the bombing.*

> *The woman in the Uddingston [host family's] house was pleasant enough as I recall, and I recall my mother saying the same about her. In my older years, I have often reflected on the absurdity of moving us to such conditions when the likelihood of getting bombed was not much greater than if we had stayed in our part of the city. Still, who knows? These were the days of obedience I suppose. Wouldn't be doing something daft like that now though.*

Gordon (from Clydebank) remembered:

All the people we stayed with treated us well but again, I think that happens if your Mum is there – she would not have been impressed if they were not!. I've thought about that over the years and how enlightened this was (Mum was with us) in a period of such madness: I mean wartime. Yeah, it was really enlightened and it impresses me every time I think about it. I would have gone mad without my Mum. Maybe she would have preferred to stay at home wthout us haha!

Although as Crosby (1986, p.43) points out, much of the imagery of the evacuees was pejorative in nature, literature is also to be found which publicly refutes the claim that all evacuated children were in poor health and socially deprived. For example, the Lord Provost of Glasgow suggested in 1940 that industrialisation in Scotland had caused an upheaval of communal life due to the preoccupation with material gain at the expense of degeneration and demoralisation of the majority (*Aberdeen University Review* 1940). Boyd (1944, p.69) supports the notion of exaggeration (of the pejorative image) regarding the evacuees and concludes that

> the great majority of the children were reasonably clean in person and on the whole there appears to have been a considerable amount of exaggeration of the evil.

As Glennie (from Glasgow) and others remembered when outlining the makeup of their families at the time:

> *Mum, Dad and five children. Our granny also lived nearby and we were very close to her. We were quite ordinary money wise and all that, but my Dad had a good job and we were pretty well looked after. My mother was a bit of a fusspot and we were always very clean. I'm not sure of the image they had of us during the evacuation thing. I didn't meet one evacuee in our evacuation village at school or anywhere who was not very clean. I have always despised that judgement by class thing. I still do.*

James (from Glasgow*):*

There were two children there a boy and a girl but they were much older than my brother and me. Both taught at St Ninian's school. I was of the impression that John [the son of the host family] *thought my brother and me were picked from the billeting area at Lenzie* [rather than from Clydebank] *because we looked 're-spectable'. This was our second Evacuation of course; the first one was just up the road from where we lived in Clydebank. The bombs could have got us easily there – what was that about?*

John again (from Clydebank):

The family lived just off Livingstone Street and near the canal bridge. We lived in a NEW Council house which made us pretty special, I mean because many of our friends lived in privately rented tenement flats. We were fine though, but so were my pals in the tenement flats. My family must have just been lucky to get up near the top of the list to get a new Council house. You might even callus middle class today haha!

Nan (from Glasgow):

We lived in a tenement flat in Broomhill [west side of Glasgow]. *It wasn't the best but we were just like everyone else. They seemed to be happy times, lots of fun with my pals cos there was no real traffic in the streets. We didn't want for much. I don't ever remember having to see a doctor. That's amazing isn't it?*

Although somewhat negatively portrayed, as the following accounts illustrate, while some residents in the country towns/farming communities were ill-disposed to the evacuees, this did not preclude the evacuated children from gaining some benefit from their time away from the urban areas where they had lived all of their lives to date. Nan clearly articulated her positive memory:

The woman grew a whole lot of vegetables which fascinated me and she was very kind and let me plant them and tend them too. I think my Mum loved that part of it. I've always been a keen gardener and I wonder if it had anything to do with the Evacuation. I've lived in Australia now for quite a while but now that you're asking me, all of that experience has come back very clearly. I must tell my children now. But maybe I'll leave it till you write the book!

Nessie (from Glasgow) recalled:

Last year when I returned to Rusko House [Gatehouse of Fleet] and it really was a dream come true for me. The countryside is so beautiful and my brother has always wished he could have retired there. Two of the other evacuees went to live in California but each time they came to Scotland, they had a trip to Gatehouse to see how the Rusko House was standing up. When I was in Gatehouse, I went to the Library and told my story of the Evacuation and it was printed in the local newspaper. However, if you go there between 1.00 and 2.00 pm, you might be the only person in the street, like I was! Later in life I caught up again with my friend Robin who was also at Rusko House and we are firm friends and often reminisce about our times there. My mother really enjoyed that time too, although she worked quite hard around the place as I recall. Woman's work.

Robin (from the West End of Glasgow) confirmed this at the interview session at which Nessie attended as follows:

Nessie is absolutely right. We had the most wonderful time and I have the best memories of that time. It's really great that Nessie and I have had this time to reflect on it all. I realise that many people did not have an experience like ours. I haven't told my story other than today, but Nessie's story is essentially mine anyway. I go back as often as I can and still feel good about my experience.

George (from Glasgow) said:

I loved the feel of that place (a small town in Ayrshire). It always seemed to be bright, not sunshine of course, just bright. Space really is so important in life and over the years I have managed to achieve a lot of space myself. Lucky me!

A complementary theme which ran through the participants' recollections was that although they all had good things to say about life in the country, they were also loyal to their own home and situation. The extent of their loyalty is rather disarming but is an important hallmark of the Scottish evacuees in their telling of their stories. They held an understanding that they crossed a social divide which they had acknowledged during their time away. But they also understood that they would return home and that life would revert to that of the pre-war period.

For example, Patricia (from Glasgow) philosophically, acknowledged a sense of disloyalty to both her own parents and the people and the place of her Evacuation. This shows a considerable level of maturity from a child who was only ten years of age at the time:

> *After being in the country for a while, I had learned so much and had enjoyed it all so much. But when it was time to go home to Glasgow, I felt quite good about it. Mind you, I did miss the country thing. Still, Scotland's not such a big place; it ended up I could have gone back to our billet almost when I wanted. For some reason I didn't though. I'm not sure that my family in Glasgow would have enjoyed me praising the place so much – might have seemed a bit ungrateful or something. But that was then and this is now.*

Patricia's reveries serve as an introduction to the next part of this chapter which allows the evacuees' narratives to paint a vivid picture of their enjoyment of the wide open spaces afforded them at their billets away from the cities.

So much Space and Other Reflections
In order to appreciate why the Scottish participants embraced their time in the country, it is important to acknowledge how life would have been during wartime had they stayed at home in the cities. To this end, the following paragraphs are taken from a retrospective published in 2005 of the war years in Scotland by the newspaper, *the Evening Times (Times Past: Glasgow at War)* which outlines the social and economic situation in the cities.

> The citizens had to get used to rationing of many of the basics of life caused by shortages. There were often blackouts

of total suburbs in order to limit the targets of severe bombing and those who worked in production lines were often obliged to work 12 hour shifts. Due to the serious shortages of most necessities, but food in particular, the citizens were exhorted to 'dig for victory'. Planting of potatoes and cabbages, which were Scottish staples, took place in flower beds, schoolyards and often bomb sites. Given that many Scots lived in city tenements which were gardenless and which were a target for bombs, it was to the allotments that many looked to help with their food requirements. A perhaps incongruous outcome of rationing was that restaurants were forbidden to charge more than five shillings for a meal, a concession meant to ensure that in this social arena at least, all had the same access to 'luxury'. This concession during rationing appears to be somewhat naïve given that five shillings would have meant little to the rich but much to those less financially well off.[9].

Little wonder then that the evacuees embraced their new surroundings to the extent that some did, especially when they were given some insights by their families and friends, into the extent of deprivation in wartime life in the cities they had left behind. As Chris (from Dundee), whose time away was not far from his own home, but which was quite different from life in the industrial city he left behind, recalled:

> I was evacuated to a farm in a place called Errol which was only about 18 miles away from Dundee and it was to friends of the family. As I said, our own house, which was very nice by the way, with three bedrooms, a kitchen, dining room and a living room and bathroom, ran alongside the main road from Aberdeen to Dundee. So when I got to the farm it was a very joyous time for me. Also, don't forget I was with family friends who were a part of my life anyway. But I was only three at the time, nearly four, but I really do remember the farmer friend taking me on haycarts and the like every day to check on the cows and the other animals around. I think he had pigs but I wasn't enchanted by them. I'm not sure whether he told me that or if I actually remember that.

Anyway, I certainly do remember that routine every morning and I loved every bit of it. But living in Dundee was not that far from the country anyway because it's not such a big city so I was always able to revisit those happy times in my imagination when I took my walks in the country after the war. The importance of family/close friends when away from home cannot be overstated, especially when a young child. No two homes are the same so it would have been very unsettling indeed if not for the family/ friends connection.

Most of the evacuees expressed their enjoyment of the physical expanse of their temporary homes, and the wonder of the adventure of the open spaces. The participants saw the countryside as a place which offered a more interesting and rich experience than that of their lives in the inner city at that time. Many recalled their excitement at the space their temporary homes provided. Others were enchanted by the smells and the bounty of the country gardens and the fields of vegetables and of course of the animals they could touch because they were just 'over the hill'. Jim, whose experience was quite different from those of most of the other participants, was evacuated to a country house quite near the town of Helensburgh which is 20 kilometres from the city of Clydebank. The country house where he and his whole family were billeted was at that time the home of very successful publishers called Blackie and Son Ltd. Jim reminisced that:

In a country house the size of Hill House, it was to be expected that there would be a huge garden. Helensburgh is also semi-rural and near the river Clyde, so there was much to do even though we were actually very near to shipyards etc. which were the target of the bombs. We children and remember there were eight of us had the life of Riley, roaming across fields and peering at cows and sheep to our hearts' content. I can never credit how our experience happened. Imagine someone with a beautiful home well it was really an estate taking on a mother and eight children, several under school age! It beggars belief. But it has ensured that I have a generous view of the world myself, although to be honest I've had a good life so I don't need to manufacture kindness. I like to tell my story every time Charles Rennie Mackintosh is mentioned anywhere and at any time. Mostly people are interested but of course Hillhouse is now listed by the National Trust for Scotland and they can go and see for themselves. I still cannot get over the fact that we were able to be a part of such a talented creation.

Jim offered insightful narratives giving a wonderful example of how strange times can emit unexpected outcomes. He was astounded that a family of his station was made so welcome by 'old money' to the extent that it was. The house had been designed by Charles Rennie Mackintosh, one of Glasgow's most renowned and respected architects who was also a furniture designer and painter[10]. This background to Jim's sojourn suggests a greater story has perhaps still to be told. Of particular moment is Jim's appreciation of the influence his Evacuation experience afforded him throughout his life.

A further happy account from quite the opposite Evacuation experience is recalled by Louise, whose mother and father hosted a family of a mother and five children from Glasgow on the family farm in the Scottish border country. Louise remembers the excitement of the evacuees and their complete lack of fear in their new surroundings. Louise was the only Scottish participant whose family had hosted evacuees, but it is evident from her narratives that her experience was a positive one. She was not only interested in the children themselves, she was also touched by the opportunity to be able to add something tangible to the lives of her lodgers:

I recall that the children were enchanted with the proximity of the farm animals and often to their cost. Sometimes they would just run towards the cows and forget that there would be a bull in there which might be less friendly than the cows. The sheep were a different matter because somehow the children were less interested in them possibly because the sheep ignored them. I recall that they really enjoyed chasing the birds around the place too. On reflection, having taken all of this for granted myself as a child, I suppose it would have been enchanting for them since they had lived in a poor area in Glasgow. These five girls were very sweet and shy, as I recall. Years later, one of the then children came to visit us and we were all rather wistful. She turned up at the farm about 15 years ago and my brother was there. She was Mary who was probably about 12 when she was an evacuee. My brother remembers it as follows:

She called at the farm, purely on chance to see if the same folks were still there. Luck was with her. She introduced herself, and I was amazed. She was even more surprised when I could remember her name. She probably stayed longer than the rest of them. Evacuees were farmed out to whoever had spare room and many places were taken over to house them too. Cally hotel in Gatehouse became a Glasgow boys' school and Lochnaw Castle was also taken over for evacuees[11].

Louise: As farm girl I had no appreciation of the lives of others in the cities but of course I had made the usual pilgrimages 'to town'; nevertheless I really had no notion of poverty in my childhood. Mind you, I don't really think those children thought they were poor: not at all. The Evacuation had a huge impact on my life.

Alec (from Glasgow), whose reflections were amusing while also being insightful, describes his billet in the country:

The first place we went to was Peterhead in the north of Scotland. That was OK but I really think different parts of Scotland do have their own culture, even considering how small Scotland is geographically speaking.

Later we went to a place called Carfin in central Scotland, about 15 miles east of Glasgow. It was a small village so it was really in the country. My brother and I were able to be let out by ourselves because I was 11 and Robert was eight and the family must have trusted us. Probably because he thought we were streetwise coming from Glasgow.

Anyway we had a very good time there roaming all over the place. We used to look for rabbits down holes but I couldn't kill them or anything. I think the people in Carfin ate them though. We were both scared of the sheep for some reason but we loved going right up to the cows. It all sounds daft now.

Interestingly, enough there is a grotto there to Lourdes (Our Lady of Lourdes) dating from 1922, and it is a pilgrimage centre. In Carfin in 1836 of 6581 only 116 were Catholics. I think that is a strange statistic because why would you build a grotto at a place where no-one local would be very interested. Something special must have happened there but I never did find out. There was a man in Carfin who had no legs and he managed to get around on skates.

Alec's recollections bring to life their country experiences and their great enjoyment of their time spent away from the city. On the whole, these show that the evacuees had very positive memories, which are quite contrary to the stereotypical image of impoverished children being billeted with disapproving and critical hosts who regarded themselves as being of a vastly superior class.

Nostalgia

The notion of nostalgia has a remarkably long written history as Natali (2004) reminds us. A 1688 tract by Johannes Hofer, a Swiss doctor, talks of the exile's wistfulness, resulting from the desire to return to one's home. But the simple desire to return home does not fully account for all the emotions and psychological factors involved in nostalgia or dystalgia: a word coined by Janack (1999, pp.34-49). Janack's 'dystalgia' is defined as an unhappy reflection on past experiences but the nostalgia experienced by most of the participants in this study, was that which evoked sentimentality rather than hurt or pain. However, one thing is clear: if one experiences nostalgia, the two ingredients of loss and disconnection are often present as well as longing and the sentiment of ambiguity. Nostalgia has many contemporary definitions including those of Muller (2006, p.739) who acknowledges that the concept of nostalgia is difficult to understand and suggests that

> even the most sophisticated of its critics acknowledge it is paradoxical. Its history shows it to have been variously treated as a physical disorder, a mental disorder, a 'mere' emotion,

and a symptom of the modern age. It involves a backward glance through history, but not toward a place or even a time that is necessarily real.

However the nostalgia experienced by the participants indicates that a carefree childhood was the experience of many; therefore, their nostalgia had a positive hue. As Stewart (originally from Edinburgh) told me:

> *My recollection of life in this new environment was my awareness of the difference of the fast city life with its tramcars and traffic on the roads to the quieter less bustling of the laidback small town, where people were more friendly. People seemed to have time to care about each other. The extent of inter communication (I do not want to use the word gossip) spread more than one's immediate neighborhood. I remember in town one day I was talking with a girl, not in our immediate neighborhood and by the time I reached home my Mother had heard that I now had a new girlfriend and who she was. The news moved faster than the pace of my walk home.*

> *I have lived in Africa for a long time now but there are some times when I go out country walking in my now Africa home terrain, for whatever reason I am transported back to that time in the Scottish countryside. It is always a pleasant recollection, not sad, just reflective..I much prefer living in a city though.*

Nevertheless, there were several instances of nostalgic ambivalence inasmuch as many could not quite understand why this was so, arguing that it was a strange notion to look back with much fondness for a time of great insecurity and danger, yet for many nostalgia is a bittersweet emotion as Jim (from Clydebank) mused – again about his time at Hillhouse:

> *…it is now a National Trust property* [Hill House] *and I reflect often how lucky we were and how much it (the billeting) might have influenced us because our life chances would have never been anything like those of residents of such a place. All eight of the children went on to lead very rich lives. We might not have made it*

had we stayed in Clydebank and would have experienced the hor-
rors of that awful Blitz. What wonderful memories.

Whilst contemplating their own nostalgic sentiments, several participants expressed disappointment that public nostalgia seemed to have as its focus the
glory and heroism of the war while neglecting the evacuees' story. Margaret
(from Clydebank) was most upset about this issue and in responding to the
question about what it was like when she went home, she replied:

> *Actually I don't remember a thing about that. But I know that 'my*
> *war experience' has hardly ever been talked about whereas the war*
> *thing in general has been done to death. I mean, movies and tele-*
> *vision programmes by the dozen. There was a programme mind*
> *you a couple of years ago I think about the Evacuation, but do you*
> *know, no-one even asked me about it even though that programme*
> *was showing at the time. I think it ran over a few weeks. I certainly*
> *think something about that. I'd like everyone to see our feelings and*
> *memories. Our stories have not been told and I hope you can do this*
> *for us.*

Nostalgia is also an easy target for ridicule: being self-indulgent and bourgeois.
An excellent example of this is the nostalgia rekindled by British television
favourites from the 1960s and 1970s such as *Dad's Army* and *It ain't half hot*
Mum which were instruments of parody in some ways mocking the sober sentiments promulgated by government agencies and the media during World
War Two. Perhaps it is not so surprising then that as recently as December
2008, the then British Prime Minister, Gordon Brown called on the people of
Britain to test their characters and to show some wartime spirit during hard
economic times; in other words they should re-create a past where the nation
pulled together in the face of adversity (Peterkin 2008, n.p.). It might well be
that his audience – those not from the war era – would surely have mocked
this sentimentality – a time of struggle and fear.

In order to reclaim their relevance, several evacuees participated in retrospec-
tives such as the War Memories Project which contributed to local publications such as those depicting the Clydebank Blitz, thereby engendering a level
of nostalgia: looking back with a fondness encompassing a level of ambiguity.

Of particular note in this regard is the commemoration of the Evacuation at St Paul's Cathedral in London on the 70th anniversary of the first Evacuation of World War Two. This commemoration gave an opportunity for evacuees and others involved in the Evacuation, to take part in a formal service organised by the Evacuees Reunion Association which was established in 1995 and has 2,200 members as at 2012. The Association is a non-profit registered charity.

For the 3.5 million children who were evacuated during the Second World War.
Formed with the support of the Imperial War Museum.

Almost without exception, the participants indicated their enjoyment of the nostalgic component of their trip down memory lane provided by this research and agreed that it is a valuable tool to record and make sense of the great Evacuation undertaking, even as late as their contribution to this work. Cathie, in recalling the bombing of her home town, Clydebank and the subsequent Evacuation, was confused about the conflicting tangents of nostalgia and replied in answer to the question: Have you ever discussed your experience in any detail before?

> *No, and there doesn't seem to be much interest in it from people generally. But I think children should be made more aware of it all at school. Lest we forget and all that. It's been good to talk about it today though. I wasn't really comfortable about the idea of talking to you but I've enjoyed thinking about it all again. I really enjoy watching the old newsreels and we had that exhibition thing a few years ago in Clydebank which brought it all back.*

> *It's funny you know that I got all nostalgic and thoughtful about the whole business because in reality they were terrible times, especially in Clydebank. Even today, if I get with my pals who are still around we talk a lot about the bravery of all the people during the blitz and when we see the pictures of it all and all those bombed buildings, we feel a bit happy and sad at the same time. I mean about the war in general but really Clydebank I think. But we should really be feeling angry I think but we don't. Another thing*

*is, in a funny way I feel the same about the Evacuation experience.
I mean a bit nostalgic in a positive way, and I'm just not sure why
because for many they really were bad times.*

For John (from Glasgow), his reflection on nostalgia was a happy evocation:

*Yes at our billet, I went to the local Primary (school) and travelled
by bus. I remember this quite clearly. My brother and I had a long,
long walk in a country road. Well, it seemed like a long, long, walk.
I have no idea how far it was. But I do recall being excited by the
fact that the river was sometimes in flood and we therefore could
not go to school. Seeing the power of nature in action was a great
excitement. I was actually happy to go to school because I don't like
things to stand still. Indeed, my life is still unstill haha! I don't walk
so far now though, but I still have a comfortable, sort of smiling
memory of those times.*

Many participants acknowledged the complexity of the power of nostalgia in
their narratives when they indicated a level of confusion when trying to understand why they would find some comfort in remembering times and events
which, it could be argued, should evince unhappy emotions. Marie's (from
Glasgow) thoughts confirm this confusion which sometimes assailed the participants as she recalled (see p. 60):

*Certainly makes me nostalgic remembering the words to that wee
song - sounds a bit daft now though -all those promises to give away
your youth and to follow, follow, follow. A big bit of indoctrination
and inducement there. I'm always a bit suspicious now about that
kind of rhetoric.*

There is no doubt that she accepted the authority of the church (a hallmark of
Scottish children's lives at the time) in all of the Girls Training Corps activities,
including recruitment.

Nevertheless, nostalgia can also be about retreat and remembering that he had
not discussed his Evacuation before, Jack (from Glasgow) explained:

No I haven't, because no-one asked me, but I can tell you I've enjoyed telling the story very much, bringing back the sweetness of it all. I really didn't realise that it had impacted on me until today; especially of my love for the countryside. Now I wonder why I just didn't up and off when I grew up, but I suppose I felt something about my mum and dad because of their disabilities [Jack's parents were deaf and dumb]. *Anyway as it turned out I married a woman who didn't fancy it but* [the impact of the Evacuation] *... made me feel like I would love to have stayed in the country. I really loved all of it. As I said, we continued to visit at every opportunity via the family and the Boys Brigade which was an important little part of my life for a while. I loved to go to see the dog on the farm which unfortunately got killed on the road one time I was there. I still could cry about that. Essentially I know I would not have had the opportunity to have the country experience if it was not for the war. Just like my mum, I got some really good things from some really bad things. It's an ill wind and all that.*

Jack's thoughts resonate with the difficulties of disengagement located by Longmate (2002, p.506):

The few months after the end of the European war, had for many civilians, a strangely unreal quality. Some were reluctant to abandon their wartime duties and though Civil Defence began to be disbanded on 1 May, and the few remaining full-time A.R.P. (Air Raid Precautions) workers were given a month's notice; some volunteers continued to visit their old Wardens Post or First Aid Post until it was actually closed down, and many Civil Defence clubs survived for years. Private citizens also often experienced a feeling of loss of purpose. A young Battersea girl, eleven when the war began, seventeen in 1945, felt that 'there was a great feeling of anticlimax ... Everything seemed dull and flat after the excitement and friendliness.' A Guildford housewife believes that 'perhaps that grand comedian Robb Wilton captured the essence of nostalgia for the times of war when he said that 'the day peace broke out' he chided his wife for not looking very cheerful, and she replied 'well, there's nothing to look forward to now. There was always the All Clear' (2002, p.506).

Pop Nostalgia

Given the many aspects of nostalgia, it is perhaps inevitable that pop nostalgia has emerged as a successful commodification of all facets of the World War Two and the participants have, to some extent also been the objects of that concept. Pop nostalgia of the war in general include posters and post-cards, an example of which is one depicting two small children smiling with the caption 'Children are safer in the country ... leave them there' and another is a pack of playing cards called 'Vacuation' illustrating the disparate variety of evacuees, teachers and hosts.

Music was also a very compelling nostalgia theme, and possibly the most poignant example is that of Dame Vera Lynn, the troops' girlfriend, and her inspiring, rousing war songs, the best known being 'The White Cliffs of Dover'. Indeed, in 2009 she became the oldest living artist to make it into the top 20 of the United Kingdom albums chart. The album was released to coincide with the anniversary of the declaration of war (*The Scotsman*, 31 August 2009). Reproductions of the war posters have been displayed and sold at various commemoration milestones of the war. These examples of iconic nostalgia illustrate well, together with other emotions resulting from their exile experiences, that nostalgia is multi-faceted and the evacuees were all captive to a greater or lesser degree to this powerful emotion in all its manifestations.

Resilience

This is a recurring theme of the evacuee experiences and there is a scholarly acknowledgement that resilience is one element of the capacity to recover from the trauma of separation and exile, in this case that of the Evacuation experiences (Schofield and Beek 2005, pp.1283-1301). Resilience as defined by Riley and Masters (2005, p.13) refers to positive adaptation in the context of past or present adversity and Rutter (1987, p.316) defines it as:

> the ability to function competently despite living or having
> lived in adversity and it includes a range of protective charac-
> teristics, such as self-esteem, self-efficacy, a sense of security,

hopefulness and reflective function, which contribute to successful and adaptation and coping.

The work of Schofield and Beck is specifically concerned with children's resilience while in foster care but has application since the people with whom children were billeted, in the absence of family, partly assumed a role similar to that of a foster parent. As Marie, a Scot (now living in Perth, Western Australia) recalls:

> *I wasn't homesick, no not at all. Possibly switched off but I was very well treated and much loved. I remember riding on a haycart, and haystacks. I remember snow in the farmyard and chilblains because I walked barefoot in the snow. But it might have been different for other evacuees who didn't have their mother with them, which I believe was the case. But it seemed most evacuees just got on with things and in particular when we went home.*

> *But if I had gone to a different situation, what would I have done? I mean if the people were unkind. I suppose we would have just had to keep quiet because we had been told so often that it (Evacuation) was all for our own good – just get on with it. I have enjoyed telling my story very much and thank you and I look forward to seeing my story in print!*

Juxtaposed against Marie's experience, the account of Joan (from Lambeth) was quite different. She had required much resilience to cope:

> *Yes, I have been able to talk about my experiences but only in the last few years due to the establishment of the Evacuation group here in Adelaide [South Australia]. This involvement and this interview have made me more confident to talk about a terrible experience in my life, not necessarily to you but just to be able to contemplate a bit further about my survival from the sadness and ignominy of those times.*

Resilience was also a significant indicator of the ability to resume everyday life for the evacuees on their return from their billets. Doris from London, now living in Adelaide, remembered:

Now that I have met so many evacuees here in Adelaide, I understand that all was not good for everyone but my experience really was a lovely one with really happy memories, but I have only been able to discuss my experience in any detail in the last few years because of the group here in Adelaide. Essentially hardly anyone was very interested, not even in the beginning, [of the Evacuation experience] *as I recall. So I suppose we just got over it, whatever that means.*

Barbara (from London), who was very philosophical about her return after the Evacuation experience reflected:

Well, it was sad and troubling because by that time I only spoke Welsh. When I went back to Hampstead, my other sisters were there and a new one as well. I don't recall having a special welcome. The issue was never discussed as I recall but then my Mother wrote to me in 1959 and told me how much she had regretted letting us go. English came back as my first language and life just carried on. So good to talk to you – I appreciate this ability to articulate my story from the distance of many years.

As Eddie Roland (in Holman 2005, p. 118) remembers:

We left the island [Jersey] as children, and returned as adults. We had lived another life, had learned to look after ourselves … it required a lot of adjustment on all our parts and, in fact, we were never really the same people after it all.

Eddie's comments compare with those of and Joyce Fry (in Holman, 2005, p.18):

It was stiff upper lip time … but I think the effects went much deeper …I sometimes get too choked to even mention them.

For Joyce to cope with such adversity was a great challenge inasmuch as she endeavoured to keep some of her more traumatic experiences to herself. This necessity had hampered her recovery as she explained when interviewed for Holman's 2005 work.

Many theorists claim that Resilience is a learning process which can meaningfully assist in trauma recovery and of course logically, resilience can occur only subsequent to adversity. Two particularly engaging examples which confirm the characteristics espoused by Ramirez, that of humour:

> Here's a story. My Mum was a Scottish bowling champion and when they were in Ballantrae two of the women went to a local dance, a bowling dance - the other woman had serious arthritis and when they were there this soldier asked my mum's pal to 'promenade' and there was a dog around the place and my mum's pal said 'No, it's a St Bernard'. It doesn't sound that funny now actually, but it must have been at the time (Nancy from Glasgow),

and

> I did all sorts of things in Carfin; for example I was a bookie's runner. Mr Dunn the farmer bred wild birds. When I think about that it sounds daft cos they couldn't be wild if you captured them could you? But sometimes things were tough and I had to be a bit 'broad shouldered' as we would say nowadays – just stuff I had to do which was alien to me coming from a city (Robert from Glasgow).

'Back to Normal'

This part of the chapter benefits from Wolf's work (2007, which is concerned with Dutch Jewish children who had been hidden from the German authorities during World War Two. Wolf's *Beyond Anne Frank* (2007), has at its core a sense of renewal based on the ability of the hidden children to reinstate their lives after spending considerable periods of time being looked after by foster parents or those who became significant others. Wolf's work has application for mine since the evacuees shared this ability as Terry (from London) points out. He, in particular, took a very bright view of things:

Well, we just fell back into our old ways but I missed the country life but didn't miss it enough to bother to move there. But then we moved again so 'home' was a few places for a few years.

Unfortunately for many, as noted above, the expectation to return to normal obviated an appropriate level of interest in what had befallen the children during their separation whether accompanied by their mothers or not. Also, some of the children of the Scottish and Dutch Evacuations were to return to domestic situations which were less affluent than their adoptive homes. When interviewed, many of the hidden children stated as Wolf has recorded:

I've been waiting for fifty years for someone to ask me about this. No one ever did; they only wanted to hear about the war (Wolf 2007, p.12).

Many of the Scottish evacuees of this research responded in a similar vein. Robert (from Glasgow) in responding to whether he had ever discussed his experiences in any detail before replied:

Not in any formal way, but I have talked a bit about it all to my own family. But they're not that interested really. I suppose it's so long ago and they don't seem to think it was a big deal. But people are still quite interested in the war generally which is a shame because they can see all those movies and read all those books but they can't see or read my story.

Win (originally from Edinburgh, now in Perth, Western Australia) recalled:

I was once asked to talk about the Evacuation at the University of the Third Age here in Perth (Australia) but I have never been interviewed like today. At the University of the Third Age (here in Perth), it generated a little bit of interest but was very informal. I haven't actually talked about it much to my own family. Because they don't ask, I'm not sure if they would be interested. And it was an amazing experience now that I think about it but, no, nobody seems very interested. It was just back to normal, whatever that was. But I've enjoyed talking to you and I wasn't sure that I would.

In expanding some disappointment of the participants return, a common experience of almost all participants was the lack of interest in the evacuees' experiences while away from home, as Margaret (from Clydebank) remembered:

> *Mum reckoned she was much less scared after the Helensburgh fiasco* [where the host had treated Margaret's Mum with little respect] *and life resumed as normal as it could, given that the country was at war. I'm not sure why Mum necessarily felt safer, but it might have been that she was close to her own Mum and with the new baby, you know, family stuff. I was only very young so anything was OK if my Mum was with me. But you are the first person to ask me about all this you know. It was such a big deal I can't believe that only now is someone asking me. I think I was aware that it was a scary time but we just got on with it - I think I mean my Mum by the way, but me too I suppose because as I said no-one has ever asked me if my experience was good, bad or indifferent.*

A contributing factor to this lack of interest can partly be explained by the acknowledgement of the sociology of a country which was reeling from the outcomes of a world war where adults were struggling to make sense of their experiences. Nevertheless, that the children returning home were upset by perceived indifference is not surprising and this disappointment was still evident more than sixty years after the event. But it should be remembered that almost seventy years ago, the development of resilience theory including its application (and value) was in its infancy.

No help around for us on return
That some evacuees have been affected more significantly than others reflects a number of aspects of resilience theories and characteristics. Indeed, some seem barely to have been affected at all. Marie (from Glasgow), for example, remembered that:

> *For some reason, we went to a coastal town in the West of Scotland called Girvan which is about 80 miles south of Glasgow and we knocked on doors and it was the month of March so still quite inclement. My Mum did the talking. Can you imagine what that*

would have been like: a big squad of us looking for accommodation in those times in a small town?

We couldn't get anywhere because it was coming up holiday times and those who had places to rent didn't want us because they had already organised lets for other people for holidays. But we met some soldiers who said they would give up their beds because they were used to sleeping in rough conditions due to their war experience which was very kind of them. I'm not sure where they went, mind you. Back to the front I suppose. Eventually we all got accommodated in a boarding house. We had very few clothes I remember and the place had a living room, two bedrooms and a kitchen. Surely we must have had a bathroom in a place like Girvan[12]?

The benefits of being with mother or of a mother's influence and support are considerable relative to the level of adversity experienced by unaccompanied exiled children and were evident in Joan's story who was evacuated without her Mum but with two sisters, aged three and aged six. Joan (from Lambeth, London) has been unable to achieve solace even at the distance of more than sixty years:

All I can remember is the experience of being away, but no announcement from my mother or anything like that that we were going anywhere. But then I was only four. I can remember everything very clearly though. I'm always glad to tell my story. It seems to make me feel a bit better when I know that other people had similar experiences. But mine was really bad because I ended up being a bed wetter and was humiliated each time it happened. What the host did was hang out the washed sheets for all in the street to see. What on earth was that about? I have enjoyed talking to you about all of this, but it still upsets me that there was no great acknowledgement of my awful experience, never mind the actual experience.

The narratives in this chapter again confirm that the evacuees' experiences were multi-faceted and sometimes contradictory, but always enlightening and historically important.

Conclusion

This chapter has confirmed that many evacuees had embraced their country stay, maintaining that their time away from their homes in the major urban centres of Scotland had been beneficial. According to their narratives, these benefits were not concerned with the accommodation or other physical conditions which were in many cases of a considerably higher standard than those of their homes in the city. Rather, their positive experiences emanated essentially from their time in rural Scotland, as a contrast to their lives in the city. Account has been taken account of the strategies utilised by the evacuees to counter some of the possible dissonance of their period of exile. To this end, the themes of nostalgia and resilience played a part in their reflection of their experiences.

The theories have been included to build on the articulated memories of the Scottish evacuees during World War Two. The reflections of the evacuees of their experiences are quite remarkable given the curious circumstances in which they found themselves: as exiles in their own country. This chapter has, by the incorporation of the narratives of the participants, identified and enabled analysis of the strategies the children used to ameliorate their occasional elements of confusion and perplexity. Those who were accompanied by their mothers acknowledged that her presence was the overwhelming element of their optimism.

CHAPTER NINE:

CONCLUSION

Ach well, I suppose it was an amazing thing and I'm glad we could help to keep another bit of World War Two history alive. Aye I'm pleased you did your research about us.

But it was a long time ago and although it was amazing, there are other amazing things that I've witnessed in my life too. It was a good experience overall but you've made me reflect more than I thought I would. I am surprised I can remember as much as I have.

Not sure it could happen today though. I don't see the mums and dads of today just letting children go to strange places and strange people. I know it would have been a different experience altogether if my mother wasn't with us (Jack from Glasgow).

Some people say if you blink while driving in that area you would miss it [Gatehouse of Fleet]. *However it still has a magic for this Glasgow Keelie* (Nessie from Glasgow).

This work has set out to tell a hitherto untold story: that of the experiences of the Scottish World War Two evacuees who went from their homes in the cities which were vulnerable to German bombing, to more safe havens in the countryside.

The hypothesis has been that the Scottish Evacuation differed from the experiences of the English/Welsh undertaking in some significant ways, and it is argued that this is demonstrated in their stories. The dearth of academic interest specific to the Scottish Evacuation has also been acknowledged. Although most were 'government' evacuees, some had made private arrangements. When the order came at 11.07 on 31 August 1939 to 'Evacuate Forthwith' nearly 176,000 children assembled and 120,000 left Glasgow within three days.

This story challenges the revisionist case on Evacuation through the honesty and frankness of the participants regarding their place in the social structure at the time of the Evacuation. This is significant and important for the future of the Evacuation story in order that it takes its place in the official records, not only the historical, but also the social.

The stories of the participants in this research have been both compelling and challenging and have provided many unexpected outcomes in terms of the causal factors underlying the Scottish experience of the Evacuation and its place during World War Two. The level of detail as the participants recalled their experiences was sometimes astonishing and their willingness to take time for reflection was a valuable component of their stories.

From the rich data, several important themes emerged which substantiate the hypothesis: that the Scottish Evacuation was different in several important ways from the English Evacuation and due to these differences, the Scottish story is worthy of this work. Because much of the Evacuation literature focussed on the English experience, this tended to assume that the Scottish and English experiences were either 'British' or indeed 'English'. However, some of the differences which existed and still exist between Scotland and the rest of the United Kingdom have been illustrated.

In particular, Scotland retained a significant degree of autonomy under the Union of Parliaments in 1707 until the 20th century. Welfare was a prominent example of this autonomy particularly as it related to the welfare of children and to that end, as noted in the Clyde Committee report (which espoused these principles) made a considerable contribution to the 1948 *British Children Act*. Of particular distinction in the approach to homeless and other needy children was that fostering of children in one family home, was preferred to institutionalisation on the basis that children's need for affection and discipline can develop more positively in a family environment.

The positive outcomes of the Scottish evacuation have been expressed repeatedly throughout this work relative to their billeting and were, it is argued, a result of the already established Scottish practice of fostering in Scotland which placed importance on children being accompanied by mother. Being accompanied by their mother, the children related their enjoyment and excitement of the Evacuation adventure.

The central research question not only addressed the Scottish Evacuation story, but also demonstrated the differences related to other Evacuations. Although relatively small, but nonetheless representative, sample of Scottish evacuees, and a much smaller group of English evacuees, their experiences were used to draw comparisons. A qualitative research methodology was preferred for an oral history which uses interviews to illustrate individual experiences (quality) rather than to gain an indication of a mass response (quantity). The value of this approach is that it has created new knowledge by collecting and analysing the memories of private individuals, many of whom had never discussed these experiences with anyone else. The new knowledge generated by this study, enabled a challenge to several hitherto untested assumptions about the Scottish evacuees. These assumptions included the notions that:

- most evacuees had negative experiences during their time away from home;
- most evacuees were dirty, neglected and malnourished;
- the perception that a collective memory is more legitimate than other memory forms, and;
- although most of the evacuees believed that their experiences had limited relevance to the greater war story, this has not been the case.

With regard to the research methodology, an amalgam of those of Interpretive Interactionism (Denzin 2001), Grounded Theory (Byrne 2001, and Critical Theory (Kincheloe 2002) were utilised. This approach allowed the Scottish Evacuation story to emerge through the participants' narratives as well as develop contemplations on the issues of the maturity of the children, that their memories were individual and personal. All were anxious that their stories will contribute to the understanding and necessity of the overhaul of social policy in the United Kingdom during and subsequent to the war.

In addition to the participants' reflections on the importance of the presence of their mother, the literature on separation from the mother cannot be understated (e.g., Barnett 2008 and Altawil 2008).

That the Evacuation had some causality relative to a new approach to the social welfare of the citizens of the United Kingdom has also become of interest to the academy through such publications and centres as the *Journal of Scottish Historical Studies* and the Research Centre for Evacuee and War Child Studies. This research complements the existing bodies of knowledge, not only of the Evacuation but to the related theories of memory, attachment and the development of social policy in the United Kingdom. These elements have not been the subject of significant research relative to the Evacuation until the past ten years, but it is evident that there is an increasing interest in developing the theories further.

The Scottish Evacuation has been studied in the context of the wider British Evacuation of children from areas deemed to be targets of enemy bombing, including private and overseas schemes. The contention that the Scottish experience has been subsumed into the 'British' experience is informed by Big Nation, Small Nation theory which posits that the history of a larger entity (or nation) is often promoted as being representative of its smaller neighbour, when in fact there may be significant differences. When given the opportunity, the Scots chose to do some things differently. To augment this position on this issue, examples have been offered of the use of the titles *British/English* when in fact the *Scots* were being discussed. These examples depict the formal default in places such as the Westminster parliament as well as in official newspaper and public accounts. Therefore can it be argued that Scotland, Wales and Northern Ireland were viewed by the dominant culture during World War Two as a component of an *English empire*, while emphasising that this was not the prevailing image the Scots had of themselves.

It was also considered important to outline the overseas elements of the Evacuation because they reflect much of the thinking of the British establishment from the second half of the 19th century until the 1970s. The idea of evacuating children to places outside Britain, often unaccompanied, was developed against the backdrop of an extended period of child migration from Britain to other parts of the world, the colonies or dominions, which included Australia, Canada, New Zealand, the Rhodesias (Northern and Southern) and South Africa. The United States of America also provided sanctuary for British children, often on the private initiatives of major companies who employed staff in the United Kingdom prior to World War Two. Although not a key focus of this work, it appears that many of the children who spent some time away from their home countries indicated that they had benefited from their overseas experiences. This concurs with the experience of Scottish children from an urban environment who went to live in rural surroundings with people of different backgrounds from themselves and who similarly related beneficial experiences. However, many of the English experiences were less beneficial.

This undertaking found that the children responded to their exile with great maturity and understanding. Some were better equipped than others due in some part to their individual disposition, to their social situation at home and most importantly, their Evacuation experiences. It also indicates that, perhaps as might be expected, the children were influenced by their foster - parents' behaviours and attitudes, the conditions of their billets and whether accompanied by their mother. Many factors were evident in their responses to their exile; these include memory, remembrance, resilience, humour, location, age and family support. All of these concepts have been of great significance to the Scottish Evacuation story. The words of the participants have constantly led from the empirical to the theoretical. For example, when I asked Betty (from Clydebank) about whether she had ever discussed her experience in any detail before, she crystallised the situation of many evacuees for me when she replied:

> *A few years ago for some reason I was part of something for the Clydebank Press but it wasn't much. I've talked a lot more to you and I've enjoyed it. Will you come back? All those memories, so clear after all.*

Surprise at their own level of recall was exhibited by several participants. Given that many of the evacuees had never been formally interviewed regarding their experiences, perhaps their recall was increased due to the opportunity to relax and let their memories flow. Betty, with others, enjoyed her moment in the sun but more so, in saying 'so clear after all' she reminded me that much of the current memory discourse engages those questions of recall and remembrance. This awakening was most poignant for both her and me due to its occurrence during the interview: almost as an emergence from a long sleep.

Resilience is a further important finding, which was demonstrated in the many and varied strategies the child evacuees called upon to survive the strangeness of their time away from home. For most of the participants in this study, their return was disconcerting, due to the fact that they found it difficult to comprehend why their family and friends, who had not been part of the Evacuation, did not seem to show any interest in their time away. The resilience called upon in this regard was due to the indifference exhibited by some family and friends about their Evacuation. This lack of interest left them with feelings of dissonance and disappointment. Yet none of the Scottish participants blamed anyone for this lack of interest but were for the most part, philosophical. For most, it was just an interruption to their lives, albeit an unusual one, and although their time away from home was not unhappy, they implicitly and explicitly recognised that a level of resilience was required when dealing with their homecoming. As Jack (from Glasgow) observed with candour in response to the question about what was it like when he went home:

it was business as usual. Nobody was very interested.

This response was repeated by many other interviewees, both Scottish and English. My findings are that the majority of the Scottish participants were accompanied by their mother or, in the case of private arrangements they stayed with close relatives who lived outside the cities. Therefore, resilience being the antecedent to adversity, the development of strategies was somewhat unnecessary for many since the presence of a mother ensured a level of protection from vulnerability given the strange situation of Evacuation. But because the participants indicated that their Evacuation was not unpleasant, does not mean that they did not suffer from homesickness or estrangements from the familiar. Jack again (from Glasgow):

On the other hand, the going home is very clear, especially the strangeness of being so excited to be home and yet to yearn for the place I had spent about four years.

The English participants, on the other hand required considerable resilience to cope with a different situation, only two of these were accompanied by a parent and one of which was a private Evacuation. They had to call on personal resources to cope. Barbara (from Port Elliot in South Australia, ex London), when I asked her how the Evacuation experience impacted on her life said that her time spent away from home had been rather negative:

> *It had a huge impact on my life and that includes:*

> *On relationships I had high expectations in all relationships of a high level of support in many areas;*

> *I was a very shy child when I got home and my parents had to help me on this issue*

> *I learned to be strong.*

As Irene (originally from Bristol) recounted, some evacuees' war experience memories especially when associated with trauma, also included the physical. Irene, for example, was faced with the possibility of losing her life.

The Evacuation literature acknowledges that social change was in the consciousness of several leaders of the country prior to World War Two (including Beveridge, Keynes and Chamberlain) (Crosby 1986; Starns (2008), and although the Evacuation was not a formal social experiment, it was indeed instrumental as a harbinger of change. Notwithstanding, the Evacuation exposed issues of poor health, overcrowding and poverty which were the perceived hallmarks of all evacuees. Importantly, as the participants pointed out, the evidence regarding evacuees' health and physical condition was often impressionistic and sometimes exaggerated. This is confirmed by the works of Boyd 1944; Parsons 1998; Cunningham & Gardner 1999. This is to be expected given the extremely complex situation which was the Evacuation. Nevertheless, in support of the contradiction of the commonly held public impression (that all evacuees' health was poor and their housing often unsanitary), most of the participants did not view themselves in any way deprived or wanting. Indeed they saw themselves as 'just the same as everyone else'. Impressionistic or otherwise, the Evacuation, together with other social imperatives, did play a part in the meaningful social changes implemented towards and subsequent to the end of World War Two. In short, a people's war had to produce a people's peace.

Naturally, some of the participants remembered more than others. But this is a common condition across age and gender and social backgrounds. I can make no judgement regarding disparities in recall across participants' narratives. Suffice to say that only one participant appeared to have any significant difficulty when responding to the questions, and all others' enthusiasm did not wane at all throughout the interviews. In fact the opposite was true. This can be gleaned from the participants' voices as they are recorded in this work, particularly with regard to their unconditional responses to my question about whether they had ever discussed their experience in detail before.

Although largely neglected, the Evacuation was an important event in recent Scottish social history, and needs to assume its rightful place in the story of Scotland, not least because, as this research demonstrates, the Scottish and English Evacuation experiences differed in several important ways, which have both historical and contemporary significance.

This research closes the gap in the history of the Scottish Evacuation during World War Two and contributes to a particular body of knowledge, a major component of which has been neglected. In informing and contributing to the ongoing investigations into mass movements of children within Britain, and from Britain to the colonies during the 20th century, and more generally to mass movements of children in other places and other times, it contributes to our understandings of trauma and loss in a contemporary world fraught with separation and exile, often within the country of birth.

One of the major outcomes which has emerged from my work has been that the Scottish participants have happy, rather than sad, memories from their Evacuation experience, but although they expressed positive reactions to the commemorative events now being undertaken, these were of limited importance to them, unless they were specific to Scotland.

Acknowledgment of Sorts of the Evacuation
As noted earlier in this work, on 1st September 2009, I was able to be present

at the commemorative service at St Paul's Cathedral in London, organised by the Evacuees Reunion Association, a formal event in its format and presentation, which attracted 2,000 people, many of whom were evacuees.

South Transept   enter by West Doors

ST PAUL'S CATHEDRAL

A Service of Thanksgiving to
commemorate the
70th Anniversary of the
Second World War Evacuation
Tuesday 1 September 2009 at 11.00
Doors open at 10.00
Please be seated by 10.45
You are requested to bring this ticket with you to gain admittance
No photography or recording is permitted in the Cathedral

It also gave the opportunity to profile the Evacuation and its importance to the war and social history of the 20th century. The various media were in attendance and the event was given space in prime time news by the major British television and radio channels as well as by social media. The opportunity was taken to announce a monument to the evacuees which will be erected outside St Paul's Cathedral in London. The monument will depict the evacuees are holding hands as they leave home to escape the bombing of London and other cities for the safety of the countryside.

Several evacuees were interviewed on the morning of the service on public radio and television as a part of many commemorations and historical reflections on the advent of World War Two across the country during the week beginning 1 September 2009. I also had the privilege of talking to some of the participants after the ceremony. Unfortunately, not many of the Scottish participants attended the ceremony by and large because they deemed it not to be important since the commemoration was held in London. I also enquired of James Roffey, Chair of the Evacuees Reunion Association, in April 2011 if he was aware of any Scottish attendees and was advised that the 'Association has only two members based in Scotland, that is despite numerous attempts to recruit more'.

Although it was clear that several physical and economic constraints were given as reasons for their lack of interest in attending the commemoration service, it was also clear that the Scottish participants saw their experiences as Scottish, not English, and there should have been a similar commemoration perhaps in Edinburgh or Glasgow. But they were enthusiastic for their story to be told in the form I had indicated. They were content that their recollections would be recorded for Scotland but they possessed no great inclination to be part of perhaps the last commemoration of the phenomenon of the Evacuation.

Through this work Scotland's Evacuation story has now become Scotland's story - a formal and very important and relevant component of the British Evacuation story.

It is also timely that the children's stories are told at this time since 2015 is a year of great commemoration of World War One specifically and of the horrors of was in general including World War Two. Indeed, until we ask - 'who knows the thoughts of a child?' we cannot know (Perry 1994).

> *Although I have not talked much about it over the years, I had always hoped to get my name in lights as it were because it was such a massive undertaking with so many children and so many stories to tell. Throughout my long life I have not been able to locate real stories from the mouths of the evacuees: plenty of other people's ideas and accounts of us, but not ours.*
>
> *You have now made* our *memories and contemplations available by this book and I am so thrilled about it.*
>
> *I'll be buying the first copy!* (**May from Glasgow**).

ENDNOTES

1   This Centre's aim is to make the Centre the pivotal hub of cross discipli-
    nary War Child research in the world. To that end the Centre has pre-
    sented several conferences and produces a quarterly journal (*The
    International Journal of Evacuee and War Child Studies*. The Centre's Di-
    rector has published and edited several books, the most recent of which is
    Children: the Invisible Victims of War, 2008. The Centre's work covers not
    only the British World War Two Evacuation, but also that of Europe. Oth-
    ers endeavours relate to the effects of war on children.

2   Operation Pied Piper was the code name coined by the Ministry of
    Health, the Board of Education and indeed accepted by those involved in
    the planning and those who participated (Gardiner 2005).

3   *Report of Committee on Evacuation*, Cmd. 5837 (July 1938) – known as the
    Anderson Report. Retrieved 2 July 2009 from http://www.ibiblio.org/hy-
    perwar/UN?UK-Civil-Social/UK-Civil-Social-7.htm

4   *Report of Committee on Evacuation*, Cmd. 5837 (July 1938), par 60.

5   The movie: The tone of this clip is typically positive, trying to reassure
    parents about Evacuation. We know now that Evacuation was a very mixed
    experience. Some children enjoyed their time in the countryside and even
    ended up staying there. At the other end of the scale there existed cases of
    exploitation, neglect, and abuse.

6   Luftwaffe attack on Glasgow and Clydeside, March 14-15, 1941:
    4 x 1000 kilo bombs (high explosive)
    51 x 500 kilo bombs (high explosive)
    335 x 250 kilo bombs (high explosive)

50 x 250 kilo bombs delayed action (high explosive)
497 x 50 kilo bombs (high explosive)
42 x 'A' bombs (parachute mines)
101 x 'B' bombs (oil bombs)

[7] Miserable/inclement

[8] Joseph Stalin was the General Secretary of the Communist Party of the Soviet Union's Central Committee from 1922 until his death in 1953.

[9] In times of such stringent rationing and shortage, one could be forgiven for being surprised that restaurants were able to function at all (*Evening Times: Times Past* 2005). See http://www.crmsociety.com/of the early 20th

[10] See Boyd in Chapter Three:

[11] A prosperous town in Ayrshire, Scotland

BIBLIOGRAPHY

Primary Sources
Archives

National Archives of Scotland

National Archives of Scotland, 1936, **ED 24/1**: Meeting of Representatives of the Home Office, the Board of Education, and the Scottish office, 2 November. Regional Commissioner's Statement: satisfactory reports'.

National Archives of Scotland, 1938, **ED 24/1**: meeting at the Scottish Education Department, 12 May.

National Archives of Scotland 1938, **24/2**: Scottish Education Department memorandum, 16 May.

A vision of Britain through time. Retrieved 20 July 2010 from: http://www.visionofbritain.org.uk/text/chap_page.jsp?t_id=SRC_P&c_id=3&cpub_id=S 1931

HH50/48   Emergency Evacuation of Civil Population
Hansard Extracts   Notes of Speech by Minister of Health.
Press Cuttings. Notes of Meetings. List of Holiday Camps,
Correspondence etc
Minutes suggest **(2/11/38)** *that Fitness Camps be established throughout the country to be used for evacuation scheme.*
Suggested review of evacuation planning. Existing plans suggested one third of the population should be evacuated: Glasgow, Edinburgh, Dundee but Clydebank not included at the time. Two per-

sons in every habitable room: England: one person in every habitable room.

18/5/1939 Secretary of State for Scotland in House of Commons

Add Clydebank, Rosyth, Dunfermline, Ardrossan, Barrhead, Cowdenbeath, Culross, Kilwining, Leven, Linlithgow, Milngavie, Saltcoats, Bearsden for Reception but not Orkney and Shetland, Ross and Cromarty, Inverness and Argyll, Aberdeen, Airdrie, Bo'ness, Burnt Island, Coatbridge, Cromarty, Dumbartin, Dunfermline, Falkirk, Gourock, Grangemouth, Greenock, Hamilton, Invergordon, Inverkeithing, Irvine, Johnstone, Kirkaldy, Motherwell, Wishaw, Paisley, Queensferry, Renfrew, Rutherglen

9/1/1939 Glasgow Herald (within HH 50/48)

Protection of citizens. Holiday camps in Scotland as part of the evacuation measures. Children and adults not engaged in essential work. Weakness in Scottish Scheme: poor housing, serious overcrowding, poor water supplied. Use of 'refugee' in Anderson's report. Use of campus supported on the basis of the concerns re Scotland's housing conditions etc.

12/1/1939 – Secretary of State for Scotland:

Survey of accommodation underway with anticipated outcome by end of February. Camps issue prominent and anticipated number of children to be evacuated 500,000. Teachers too and the first mention of children.

18/1/39 Anderson

One million pounds for construction of camps   50   to be school camps in peacetime

Minister for Health: Glasgow

Children first 'Press Forward' with notion of evacuation 'No one could deny that to remove children from congested or dangerous areas was 'good'. Also discussed: Contributory pension Scheme, hospital beds, blankets.

31/8/1939 Department of Health Scotland Circular 6
Very beginning of evacuation debates. Survey of accommodation to be completed by 28/2/1939.

2/9/1939 Department of Health Scotland Circular 82
New scheme to send unaccompanied children proposed

13/9/1939 Department of Health Scotland Circular 90
Discussed how to deal with diseased children

19/9/1939 Department of Health Scotland Circular 5
Further evacuation, transport, disease, clothing, small groups: no 'mass movement.

20/9/1939 Department of Health Scotland Circular 13
Limited reference to teachers/helpers

24/10/1939 Department of Health Scotland Circular 47
Accommodation for expectant mothers
Government memo:
Lists rooms for maternity homes   amazingly comprehensive
10 bed mackintoshes
6 enamel boxes
4 pairs non-tooth dissecting forceps
2 two gallon enamel jugs

16/11/1939 Department of Health Scotland Circular 59
Concern re going home
Many billets not utilised
Frequent visits by relatives have retarded the process of settling in ...not to provide special facilities which would encourage frequent visits. Discussion physical health but not mental health.

27/12/39 Department of Health Scotland Circular 89
Encouraging pre-school children to accompany expectant mothers

27/6/1940 Department of Health Scotland Circular 263
Evacuation still voluntary but if deemed necessary will be enforced

12/10/1940 Department of Health Scotland Circular 263
Billetting of persons from England. Evacuation areas under private arrangements; allowed to be billeted with special places in England and amended from time to time

28/2/1941 Department of Health Scotland Circular 54
Reimbursements to receiving areas including private

General Defence Regulations 1939   comments
Only talk of mothers
National duty re billeting
Need to know what to do: hosts
Can't really say 'no'
'the occupier' = the husband/male
Distribution of the children
Re-imbursement a big issue
Huge bureaucracy re travel billeting, rations, recovery of costs, petrol coupons, rations books, ID cards
Planning extremely detailed
All circulars commenced 'I am directed by the Secretary of State for Scotland
Priority of classes changed over time
Several 'categories' requested inclusion, ie non able bodied older citizens
Also disputes about 'adult cripples' entitlements
Rejected applications by over 65s and infirm persons re inclusion in evacuation
'class' and priority
Use of term 'refugees'
'self-evacuees' should not move at the same time as government evacuees
National unity
'national effort', 'imagination and sympathy', 'a credit to their school', 'tolerance', 'resolution and enterprise'

HH50/108   **21/6/1939 Compulsory Reservation of Premises and other matters**

Re-confirmed the government's policy in regard to the civilian population   conclusion reached that it would be impracticable to prohibit the movement of persons not covered by the government scheme.

Not to advise people in vulnerable areas to stay put until official evacuation was carried out.

Statistics regarding available accommodation and appropriateness of accommodation. Shift in responsibility to local authorities.

HH50/109   **Public Information Leaflet 3**

Suggests that areas other than London are less likely to be heavily raided, therefore limit encouragement to evacuate. Shortage of accommodation in Scotland and that the need for evacuation is greater in the more congested areas of cities.

HH50/54   **27/8/1939 Evacuation of Civil Population**

Requisition powers
To be dealt with under Section 59 of Civil Defence Act 1939.

National Archives other than Scotland

The National Archives Learning Curve. Retrieved: October 8, 2005 from: *http://www.spartacus.schoolnet.co.uk/2Wwevacuation/htm*

National Archives of Australia, 'The role of non-government organisations'. Retrieved: 8 December 2008 from http://www.naa.gov.au/Publications/research_guides/guides/immig/pages/chapter10.htm

National Archives.gov.uk. Parliamentary Debates, 5th Series, 1939-40, vol. 361. Retrieved: 12 January 2011.

National Archives United Kindgom. Retrieved: 5 August 2009 from http://yourarchives.nationalarchives.gov.uk/index.php?title=Children's_Overseas_Reception_Board.

Newspapers (chronological order)

'Regret at condition of evacuees', 1939, *The Glasgow Herald*, 21 April, p.8.

'Scottish school children moved to safety', 1939, *The Glasgow Herald*, 2 September, p.12.

'Fewer leave Glasgow than expected', *The Glasgow Herald*, 2 September, 1939, p.13.

'Reception areas' welcome for evacuated', 1939, *The Glasgow Herald*, 2 September, p.14.

'The billeting of evacuated persons', 1939, *The Glasgow Herald*, 11 September, p.5.

The Scotsman, 1939, 15 September, p.6 (cited in J.Stewart and J. Welshman 2006, p.108.

'Rural Districts may refuse further evacuees', 1939, *The Glasgow Herald*, 16 September, p.4.

'Private evacuees house in Renfrewshire, 1939, *The Glasgow Herald*, 23 September, p.6.

Glasgow Herald 1939, 24 September, p.8.

'Further Glasgow evacuations', 1939, *The Glasgow Herald*, 20 October, p.8.

'Scotland's wartime problems – how human factor could help with Evacuation difficulties', 1939, *The Glasgow Herald*, 22 November.

'The trek back of evacuees', 1939, *The Glasgow Herald*, 24 November.

'Scottish evacuated children: Regional Commissioners Statement – Satisfactory reports, 1940, *The Glasgow Herald*, 9 January, p.8.

'Evacuated children and holidays – urged to remain in Reception areas', 1940, *The Glasgow Herald*, 17 June, p.8.

'Evacuation of children: responsibility for cleanliness', 1941, *The Glasgow Herald*, 4 July, p.9.

'New evacuation areas, Greenock, Port Glasgow and Dumbarton', 1941, *The Glasgow Herald*, 30 July, p.9.

'Evacuation of children – government to stop abuse of system, 1941, *The Glasgow Herald*, 29 October, p.5.

Later Newspapers alphabetical order

Annear, R. 2008 in R. Sorensen, 'True Blue Tales', *Weekend Australian Review*, 26-28 January, p. 4.

Maklin, J. 'Apology will address terrible wrongs: Macklin', *The Australian.* Retrieved: 28 October 2009 from: http://www.theaustralian.news.com.au/story/0,,26002367-2702,00.html

BBC Scotland 2007, 'Scottish Election 2007'. Retrieved: 8 May 2007 from: http://news.bbc.co.uk/1/hi/uk_politics/scotland/default.stm.

Bloomfield, B. 2009, 'Blitz children to get their own one million pound memorial at St Paul's, *London Evening Standard*, 21 July, p.4.

'Britain says sorry to child migrants', 2010 *The West Australian*, 25 February, P.14

Burnside, I. 2011, 'Remembering Clydebank Blitz', *the Scotsman*. Retrieved: 17 March 2011 from: http://www.scotsman.com/spectrum/Remembering-Clydebank-blitz.6729378.jp

'Clydebank remembers its dead 70 years after Blitz', *The Herald*. Retrieved: 24 March 2011 from http://www.heraldscotland.com/news/home-news/clydebank-remembers-its-dead-70-years-after-blitz-1.1090204

Doogue, G. 2011, 'Those for whom the war is finally over', *The West Australian*, 12 August, p.13.

Dyer, C. 2000, 'A challenge to the Crown: now is the time for change', *Guardian.co.uk*, December 6.

Ham, P. 2008, in R. Sorensen, 'True Blue Tales', *Weekend Australian Review*, 26-28 January, p.4.

Heffer, S. 2009, 'England pays for the luxury of Scottish values', *The Telegraph*, 9 September, p.12.

Peterkin, T. 2008, 'Brown urges Britons to show some wartime spirit during hard times', *Scotsman*, December 28.

Roberts, L. 2009, 'Saved by the Pied Piper', *Daily Record*, 29 August, pp.17-18

'Rural districts may refuse further evacuees', *The Glasgow Herald*, September 23, 1939.

'SNP hails increased support for Scottish independence', 2009, The Herald, January 7, p. 8.

Walker, P. 2009, 'Brown to apologise to care home children sent to Australia and Canada, 18 November, *The Guardian*. Retrieved: 23 February 2011 from: http://www.guardian.co.uk/society/2009/nov/15/apology-child-migrants-gordon-brown

'Wartime sweetheart Dame Vera meets chart success again', 2009, *The Scotsman*, 31 August. Retrieved: 4 November 2009 from http://thescotsman. scotsman. com/entertainment/Wartime-sweetheart-Dame-Vera-meets. 5601927.jp

Westward Ho! 'Focus on Film'. Retrieved: 10 January 2010 from: http://www. nationalarchives.gov.uk/education/focuson/film/film-archive/player.asp?catID=2&subCatID=7&filmID=15

Personal Communications

Gardner, C. 2009, Scottish Government, on behalf of A. Salmond, First Minister, Scottish Government.

Roffey, J. 2009, *Evacuees Reunion Association*, 24 February 2009.

Roffey, J. 2011 *Evacuees Reunion Association*, 24 April.

Scottish Newspapers, August 2009.

(See Appendix Three)

Acts of Parliament

The Scotland Act 1998. Retrieved: 4 October 2007, from http://www.scotland. gov.uk/About/18060/11550

The United Nations Convention on the Rights of the Child. Adopted and opened for signature, ratification and accession by General Assembly resolution 44/25 of 20 November 1989 *entry into force* 2 September 1990, in accordance with article 49.

Union of the Crowns of 1603, and the *Acts of Union* of 1707.

Retrieved: 27 October 2007 from: http://www.alba.org.uk/.

University of Aberdeen, 2007, 'Elections in the Czech Republic'. Retrieved: 12 February 2008 from http://www.abdn.ac.uk/cspp/crelec.shtml.

Convention on the Rights of the Child, 1990, Office of the High Commissioner for Human Rights. Retrieved: 5 July 2006 from: http://www.unhchr.ch/ html/menu3/b/k2crc.htm.

Secondary Sources

Aberdeen University Review, in J. Stewart and J. Welshman, 2006 'The Evacuation of children in wartime Scotland, Culture Behaviour and Poverty, *Journal of Scottish Historical Studies*, Iss. 26, vol. 1. pp. 100 – 120.

A child migration timeline. Retrieved: 26 February 2006 from: http//:www. goldonian.org/Barnardo/child_migration.htm.

Adam, R. 1975, *A Woman's Place*, Chatto & Windus, London.

Addison, P. 1975, *The road to 1945: British politics and the Second World War*, Cape, London.

Ainsworth, M.D., Blehar, M., Waters, E. & Wall, S. 1978, *Patterns of attachment: a psychological study of the strange situation*, Erlbaum, New Jersey.

Allen, J. and Dougherty, B. 2006, 'Recovering a lost history using Oral history: The US Supreme Court's historic Green v New Kent County, Virginia, *The Oral History Review*, Summer/Fall, vol. 33, Iss. 2.

Allsop, R. 2006, 'Do we need more history summits', *Public Affairs Review: A Quarterly Review of Politics and Public Affairs*, Vol. 58, Iss. 4, December. Retrieved: 15 May 2008 from Informit database.

Altawil, M. 2008, 'The effects of chronic war trauma among Palestinian children' escaped' in M. Parsons (ed) *Children: the invisible victims of war*, DSM Technical Publications Ltd. Peterborough.

Anderson, B. 1991, *The imagined community: reflections on origin and spread of nationalism*, Verso, London.

Banks, H. 1944, 'Child Evacuation in Scotland in WWII'. Retrieved: 21 July 2005, from: http://www.lib.gcal.ac.uk/heatherbank/pdfs/Childevacuation.pdf.

Barnett, R. 2008, 'Children of the Nazi Holocaust: the ones who escaped' in M. Parsons (ed) *Children: the invisible victims of war*, DSM Technical Publications Ltd. Peterborough.

BBC.co.uk, *Modern Scotland*. Retrieved: 10 July 2008 from: http://www.bbc.co.uk/history/Scottishhistory/modern/intro_modern2.sh2ml.

BBC History, Daily Mirror's coverage, Saturday, 2 September 1939.

Retrieved: 19 June 2005 from:

http://www.bbc.co.uk/history/war/wwtwo/evacuees_04.shtml

Beasley, M. 2007, 'Telling the past', *The Weekend Australian Review*, April 14-15, p.2.

Becker, A. 2005, 'Memory gaps: Maurice Halbwachs, memory and the Great War', *Journal of European Studies*, Iss. 35, pp. 102 – 113. Retrieved: 13 March 2008 from SAGE Publications database.

Birtchnell, J. & Kennard, J. 1984, 'How do the experiences of the early separated and early bereaved differ', and to what extent do such differences affect outcome', *Social Psychiatry*, vol. 19, pp. 163 – 171.

Black, J. 2007, *The Second World War, Volume V1 Causes and Background*, Ashgate, Aldershot.

Bleich, D. 2003, 'Finding the right word' in D.P. Freedman & O. Frey, *Autobiographical Writing across the disciplines*, Duke University Press, Durham and London.

Borland, K. 2000, 'That's not what I said': interpretive conflict in oral narrative research', in A. Turnbull, 2000, 'Collaboration and censorship in the oral history interview', *International Journal of Social Research Methodology*, vol. 3, no. 1, pp. 15-34. Retrieved: 12 January 2007 from Taylor & Francis database.

Bouma, G. and Atkinson, G (eds) 1995, *A handbook of Social Science Research*, Oxford University Press, Oxford.

Boyd, W. 1944, *Evacuation in Scotland*, University of London Press, London.

Boyd, W. 2006, *Restless*, Bloomsbury, London.

Boym, S. 2001, *The future of nostalgia*, Basic Books, New York.

Briggs, S. 1975, *Keep smiling through*, Weidenfeld and Nicolson, London.

Britannia Online. Retrieved: 26 February 2008 from: http://www.britannica. com/eb/topic-179845/Edwardian-era.

British Government, *National Statistics*. Retrieved: 29 September 2007 from: http://www.statistics.gov.uk/census2001/profiles/64.asp.

Britten, N. 1995, 'Qualitative Research: Qualitative interviews in Medical Research, *British Medical Journal*, 311(6999): 251, 22 July.

Brown, M. 2000, *Evacuees: Evacuation in wartime Britain 1939 – 1945*, Sutton Publishing, Stroud.

Bryman, A. 2008, *Social Research Methods*, Oxford University Press, Oxford.

Buettner, E. 2006, 'Cemeteries public memory and Raj, nostalgia in post-colonial Britain and India, *History and Memory*, vol. 18, Iss. 1, pp. 5 – 44.

Calcott, D. 2001, *Windows*, Fairbridge Marketing Company Limited, Christchurch, New Zealand.

Calder, A. 1969, *The People's War*, Pantheon Books, New York.

Calder, A. 1999, 'Beneath the high-rise estates of urban Scotland lies the enduring land', *The Independent*, 6 March.

Campbell, M. And Gregor, F. 2002, *Mapping Social Relations: a primer in institutionalised ethnography*, Garamond Press, Ontario.

Childs, D. 1995, *Britain since 1939*, MacMillan Press, London.

Collins Dictionary, 1991, Harper Collins, Sydney.

Colvin, I. 1971, *The Chamberlain Cabinet*, Taplinger Publishing Company, New York.

Commonwealth of Australia 2001, *Lost Innocents: Writing the Record, Report of Child Migration*, Senate Printing Unit, Parliament House, Canberra.

Connerton, P. 1989, *How societies remember*, Cambridge University Press, Cambridge.

Connerton, P. 1993, 'Remembering and forgetting', *Commonwealth Center for Literary and Cultural Change Seminar*, University of Virginia, USA, 27 January.

Corbin, J. & Strauss, A. 1990, 'Grounded theory research: Procedures, canons, and evaluative criteria, *Qualitative Sociology*, vol. 13, pp. 13-21.

Coser, L. 1992, 'The revival of Sociology of Culture: the case of collective memory', *Sociological Forum*, vol. 7, No. 2, pp. 365 – 372.

Cowley, E. 2007, 'Looking back at an experience through rose coloured glasses'

Journal of Business Research, Vol. 61, Iss. 10, pp. 1046-1052. Retrieved: 12 November 2008 from Science Direct database.

Crane, S.A. 1996, '(Not) writing history: rethinking the intersections of personal history and collective memory with Hans von Aufsess, *History and Memory*, June 30, vol. 8, Iss. 1. Retrieved: 13 March 2008 from Proquest database.

Crane, S.A. 1997, 'Writing the individual back into collective memory', *The American Historical Review*, vol. 102, no. 5, pp. 1372 – 1385. Retrieved: 25 March 2008 from Jstor database.

Crosby, T.L. 1986, *The impact of civilian evacuation in the Second World War*, Croom Helm, Sydney.

Cunningham P. & Gardner, P. 1999, 'Saving the nation's children: teachers, wartime evacuation in England and Wales and construction of national identity', *History of Education*, vol. 28, no. 3, pp. 327-337.

Davies, A. 1998, 'Street gangs, crime and policing in Glasgow during the 1920s: the case of the Beehive Boys', *Social History*, vol. 23, no. 3, October.

De Courcy, 1989, *1939, The last season*, Thames and Hudson, London.

de Mause, L. 1988, 'On writing childhood history', *The Journal of Psychohistory*, Iss. 16, No. 2, Fall.

Denzin et al. 2000, *Handbook of qualitiative research*, Sage Publications, London.

Desai, K. 2006, *The inheritance of loss*, Penguin, Victoria.

Department of Foreign Affairs, Republic of the Philippines. Retrieved: 28 October 2009 from: shttp://dfa.gov.ph/?p=8203.

Devine, T.M. & Finlay, R.J. 1996, *Scotland in the Twentieth Century*, Edinburgh University Press, Edinburgh.

Douglas, 1978, *The advent of war, 1939-40*, Macmillan Press, London.

Dunbar, R.I.M. 1996, *Grooming, gossip and the evolution of language*, Faber and Faber, London.

Duvenage, P. 1999, 'The politics of memory and forgetting after Auschwitz and apartheid', *Philosophy and Social Criticism*, 25; 1. Retrieved: 17 February 2008, from Sage Publications.

Education in Scotland. Retrieved: 9 January 2007 from: http//www.en.allexperts.com/e/e/ed/education_in_scotland.htm

Eley, G. 2001, 'Finding the people's war: Film, British collective memory, and World War Two, *American Historical Review*, Vol. 106, No. 3, pp. 818-838.

Elkins, R. 1997, *Male Femaling: A Grounded Theory Approach to Cross-Dressing and Sex-Changing*, Routledge, New York.

Embassy of the Republic of Poland. Retrieved: 27 October 2009 from http://www.washington.polemb.net/index.php?document=773

England, 2010. Retrieved: 10 January 2011 from: http://www.kidport.com/reflib/worldgeography/england/england.htm

Evacuation Reunion Association 2009. Retrieved: 18 February 2009 from http://www.evacuees.org.uk/index.asp.

Evans, G. 2008, Burma/Myanmar: "Facing Up to Our Responsibilities", *The Guardian*. Retrieved: 30 September from http://www.crisisgroup.org /home/index.cfm?id=5430.

Evening Times: Times Past. 2004, 'The story of Glasgow in Pictures: Part Twelve – Glasgow at War', 21 September.

Faber, D. 2008, 'Munich', *Open Letters Monthly, Munich*, Simon & Schuster, London.

Publications,Thousand Oaks.

Fara P. & Patterson, K. (eds) 1998, *Memory*, Cambridge University Press, Cambridge.

Feldman, M. 1995, *Strategies for Interpreting Qualitative Data*, Sage

Finlay I. 2003, 'St Andrews Day broadcast: BBC 1944' in S. Rose, *Which people's war?*, Oxford University Press, Oxford.

Foddy, W. 1993, *Constructing Questions for Interviews and Questionnaires*, Cambridge University Press, Cambridge.

Forgottenaustraliansourhistory. Retrieved: 22 December 2009 from: http://forgottenaustralianshistory.gov.au/apology.html.

Foster, D., Davies, S. & Steele, H. 2003, 'The evacuation of British children during World War II: a preliminary investigation into the long-term psychological effects', *Aging and Mental Health*, September, Issue 7, pp. 398 – 408.

Fraser, D. 1984, *The Evolution of the British Welfare State*, MacMillan Press, London.

Freedman, J.R. 1999, *Whistling in the dark*, University Press, Kentucky.

Fulton, R. 1999, *Is it that time already?'*, Black and White Publishing, Glasgow.

Gardiner, J. 2005, *The children's war,* Portrait, London.

Gedi, N. & Elam, Y. 1996, 'Collective Memory: what is it?', *Journal of History and Memory*, Vol. 8, Iss. 1, p.30.

General Register office for Scotland. Retrieved: 18 January 2007 from: http://www.gro-scotland.gov.uk/statistics/library/index.html

Geography British Isles. Retrieved: 4 February 2009 from: http://www.geograph.org.uk/photo/48071

Gilbert, B. 1971, 'British Social Policy and the Second World War', *Albion: A quarterly journal concerned with British Studies.* Retrieved 1 August 2009, from JStor database.

Gilligan, R. 2003, 'Promoting resilience in children and young people', *Developing Practice*, Summer.

Glaser, B.G. & Strauss, A.L. 1967, *The discovery of grounded theory: Strategies for qualitative research*, Aldine, Chicago.

Goody, J. 1998, 'Memory in oral tradition' in P. Fara and K. Patterson, *Memory*, Cambridge University Press, Cambridge.

Gordon, M. 2005, 'Memory and Performance in staging *The Line*, in Milwaukee: a play about the bitter Patrick Cudahy Strike of 1987-1989' in D. Pollok, *Remembering: Oral History Performance*, Palgrave MacMillan, New York, USA.

Grafton, B. *The Phoney War.* Retrieved: 7 August 2006 from:

http://www.militaryhistoryonline.com/wwii/bombercommand/phoneywar.aspx

Gunter, B. and Furnham, A. 1998, *Children as consumers: a psychological analysis of the young people's market*, Routledge, London.

Guttman, J. 2000, 'A letter from a reader reminds us that interviews are not necessarily the same as history features', *Military History*, vol. 16, Iss. 6, pp. 1 – 3. Retrieved: 2 February 2008 from Proquest database.

Haebich, A. 1992, *For their own good: Aborigines and government in the South West of Western Australia from 1900 – 1940*, UWA Press, Perth.

Haesly, R. 2005, 'Rue Britannia or Rule Britannia: British identities in Scotland and Wales' *Ethnopolitics*, Vol. 4, No. 1, pp. 65-83.

Halbwachs, M. 1980, *The Collective Memory*, translated by F.J. & V.Y. Ditter, Harper Colophon, New York.

Halbwachs, M. 1992, *On collective memory*, University of Chicago Press, Chicago.

Hall, C. 1998, 'Turning a blind eye': memories of empire, in P. Fara and K. Patterson, *Memory*, Cambridge University Press, Cambridge.

Hamouda, OmF. and Smithin, J.N. 1988, *Keynes and Public Policy after fifty years, Volume 1 Economics and Policy*, New York University Press, New York.

Hancock, W.K. HyperWar United Kingdom Official Histories. Retrieved: 29 September 2006 from: http://www.ibiblio.org/hyperwar/UN/UK/index.html

Hartley J. 1994, *Hearts undefeated, Women's writing of the Second World War*, Virago Press, London.

Hartley, L.P. 1953, *The go-between*, Penguin, London.

Harvey, C.T. 2004, *Scotland and Nationalism: Scottish society and politics, 1707 to the present*, Routledge, London.

Heinl, P. 2001, *Splintered innocence – an intuitive approach to war trauma*, Brunner-Routledge, East Sussex.

Heinl, P. 2006, 'A plea for recognition of childhood trauma due to tyranny, war and evacuation: The heavy burden of their unseen psychological wounds', *The International Journal of evacuee and war child studies*, December, vol. 1, No. 4, pp.61-65.

Heinl, P. 2008, 'A new world rising from the ashes: the recognition of the 'disease' of childhood war trauma, its transgenerational transmission and role as a pacemaker of change', in Parsons (ed), *Children: the invisible victims of war*, DSM, Peterborough.

Henderson, M. 2008, 'North American Evacuation: A good idea or a bad mistake' in M. Parsons, *Children: the invisible victims of war*', DSM, Peterborough.

Hendrick, H. 2003, *Child welfare: historical dimensions, contemporary debate*, Policy Press, Bristol.

Herman, A. 2001, *How the Scots invented the Modern World*, Three Rivers Press, New York.

Hill, D. 2007, *The forgotten children, Fairbridge farm school and its betrayal of Australia's child migrants*, Random House, Australia.

Hillman, J. 1992, 'Abandoning the child', in C. Jenks, *The sociology of childhood*, Gregg Revivals, Aldershot.

Hinton, J. 2002, *Women, social leadership and the Second World War: continuities of class*, Oxford University Press, Oxford.

History in Focus, 1996. Retrieved: 17 June 2005, from: http://www.history.ac.uk/ihr/Focus/War/londonEvac.html.

History Learning Site. Retrieved: 5 June 2009 from: http://www.historylearningsite.co.uk/treaty_of_versailles.htm

Holman, B. 1995, *The Evacuation: A Very British Revolution*, Lion Publishing, Oxford.

Hopkins, E. 1994, *Childhood Transformed*, Manchester University Press, Manchester.

Horn, P. 1989, *The Victorian and Edwardian School Child*, Sutton Publisher, Stroud.

Hughes, J. 2000, *Pier 21*, Retrieved: 13 February 2006, from:
http://www.pier21.ca/?supportpier21.

Hughes, J. 2007, 'The origins of World War Two in Europe: British deterrence failure and German expansionism' in J. Black *The Second World War: Volume V1 Causes and Background*, Ashgate, Hampshire.

Huxley, E. 'Atlantic Ordeal' in M. Parsons 2008, *Children: the invisible victims of war*, DSM, Peterborough.

Jackson, A. 2006, *The British Empire and the Second World War*, Hambeldon Continuum, London.

Janack, J.A. 1999, 'The future's foundation in a contested past: Nostalgia and dystalgia in the 1996 Russian Presidential campaign, *The Southern Communication Journal Memphis*, Vol. 65, Iss. 1, pp. 34 – 49.

Jenks, C. 1992, *The sociology of childhood*', Gregg Revivals, Aldershot.

Johnson, M. 2007, Book Review, 'Memory, History, Forgetting' by Paul Ricoeur, *Anglican Theological Review*, Winter, Vol. 89, Iss. 1, pp. 105 – 113.

Kaven, P. 2006, 'The political consequences in Finland or the unexpected results of the evacuation of Finnish children to Sweden during World War Two', *The International of Evacuee and War Child Studies*, December, Vol. 1, No. 4.

Kenna, R. 1996, *Scotland's children in pictures*, Argyll Publishing, Glendaruel.

Keynes, J.M. 1936, 1977, 2nd edition, *General theory of employment, interest and money*, Routledge, New York.

Kindertransport Association. Retrieved: 11 January 2011 from: http://www.kindertransport.org/history04_Britain.htm

King, E. 1993, *Glasgow's women*, Mainstream Publishing, Edinburgh and London.

Kirkwood, E. 2009, 'Stalin's return', *Prospect Magazine*, March.

Klein, K.L. 2000, 'On the emergence of Memory in historical discourse', *Representations*, Winter, pp. 127 – 150.

Kleinman, A. & Kleinman, J. 1994, 'How bodies remember: social memory and bodily experience of criticism, resistance, and deligitimation following China's Cultural Revolution, *New Literary History*, vol. 25, 25th Anniversary Issue (Part 1), Summer, pp. 707-723. Retrieved: 1 June 2006 from Jstor database.

Knox, W.W. n.d. 'Poverty, income and wealth in Scotland 1840-1940'. Retrieved: 21 January 2011 from: http://www.scran.ac.uk/

Krips, V. 2000, *The presence of the past*, Garland Publishing, London.

Kroger, M. 2004, 'Child Exiles: a new research area?', *Shofar*, Fall, vol. 23, no. 1.

Kynaston, D 2007, *Austerity Britain 1945 – 51*, Bloomsbury, London.

LaCapra, D. 2001, *Writing history, writing trauma*, The John Hopkins University Press, London.

Lamont, S. 2001, *When Scotland ruled the world*, Harper Collins, London.

Lanz, H. 1936, 'Metaphysics of gossip', *International Journal of Ethics*, Vol. 35, No. 4, pp. 492 – 499.

Lawson, F. 2006, 'How has Children's War literature changed from World War Two and development into the present day? To what extend has this shaped our views on the war child experience?' *The International Journal of Evacuee and War Child Studied*, Dec. 2006, vol. 1 No. 4.

Lee, Y. Lee, H. and Tsai, S. 2007, 'Effects of post-cue interval on intentional forgetting', *British Journal of Psychology*, Iss. 98, pp. 257 – 272.

Leeke, M. 2003, *UK Election Statistics: 1945-2003*, House of Commons Research Paper 03/59, House of Commons Library, London.

LeGros, C. & Toms, RW. 1940, 'Evacuation - Failure or Reform?' Fabian Tract 249, in A. Calder, *The People's War*, Pantheon Books, New York, p. 39.

Linklater, A. 2010, Review of Juliet Gardiner, *The Blitz: the British under attack*, *The Spectator*, 9 October.

Livingstone, S. 1998, *Seen and not heard, Scottish children 1844 – 1944*, Hamilton, Scotland.

Lodge, D. (ed) 1988, *Modern criticism and theory*, Longman Group UK Limited, Essex.

Lofland, J. 1971, *Analysing Social Settings*, Wadsworth Publishing Company, Belmont.

Longmate, N. 2002, *How we lived then: a history of everyday life during the Second World War*, Ramdom House, London.

Lowe, R. 2003, 'A Scottish diaspora: influences on education planning in twentieth-century England', *History of Education*, vol. 32, no. 3, pp. 319-330.

Lummis, T. 1987, *Listening to History: the authenticity of oral evidence*, Hutchinson, London.

Luthar, S., Cicchetti, D., & Becker, B. 2000, 'The construct of resilience: A critical evaluation and guidelines for future work', *Child Development*, Iss. 71, pp. 543 – 562.

Lynch, M. 1992, *Scotland, a new history*, Pimlico, London.

MacDonald, G. 2005, 'Why does social exclusion hurt?', American Psychological Association, Vol. 131 (2), pp. 202 – 223. Retrieved: 25 March 2008, from OVIDspTip.

MacDonald, H. 2006 'Boarding Out and the Scottish Poor Law, 1845 – 1914, *Scottish Historical Review*, LXXV, No. 2.

Macnicol, J. 1986, 'The effect of the evacuation of school children on official attitudes to state intervention', in H.L. Smith, (ed), *War and Social Change: British Society in the Second World War*, Manchester University Press, Manchester.

MacPhail, I.M. 1974, *The Clydebank Blitz*, West Dunbartonshire Libraries and Museums, Glasgow.

MacRobert, J. Clerk of the Peace, 1943, 'Juvenile Delinquency survey-Summary of findings and recommendations [Study in Ayrshire], 8 September, NAS HH 60/431. Report on Juvenile Delinquency in Glasgow.

Magnusson, M. 2000, *Scotland, the story of a nation*, Harper Collins, London.

Mandel, E. 1986, *The Meaning of the Second World War*, Thetford Press, Norfolk.

Marshall, C. & Rossman, G.B. 1999, *Designing Qualitative Research*, Sage Publications, London.

Marwick, A. 1974, *War and social change in the 20th century*, Penguin, London.

May, E.R. 2006, 'Between the Wars', 2006. Retrieved: 19 February 2006, from Grolier Online, http://www.grolier.com.wwii/wwii_2.htlm.

McArthur, A. and Long, H.K. 1935, *No mean city*, Neville Spearman, London.

McCallum, B.T. 1987, 'The contribution of Keynes after 50 years', *The American Economic Review*, May, 77, 2. Retrieved: 9 March 2006, from Proquest database.

McCrae, M. 2003, *the National Health Service in Scotland: Origins and Ideals, 1900-1950*, Tuckwell Press, East Linton.

McCrone, D. 2001, *Understanding Scotland, the Sociology of a Nation*, Routledge, London and New York.

McKenzie, T. n.d., *The Clydebank Story*. Retrieved: 25 May 2007 from: http://www.theclydebankstory.com/story_TCSB01.php.

Meeropol, A. 2008, 'Strange Fruit', *New Internationalist*, Jan/Feb, Iss. 408, p. 23.

Mesoudi, A. 2006, 'A bias for social information in human and cultura transmission', *British Journal of Psychology*, vol. 97, no. 3, pp. 405 – 423.

Misztal, B. 2003, *Theories of Social Remembering*, Maidenhead: Open University.

Modlock, S. 2006, 'Where the UK's richest people live'. Retrieved: 25 May 2009 from: http://money.uk.msn.com/guides/salarycentre/article.aspx?cp-

Moore, M.T. 1994, *Quotable Women*, Running Press, Philadephia.

Morton-Williams, J. 1993, *Interviewer Approaches*, Dartmouth Publishing Company Ltd, Aldershot.

Muller, A. 2006, 'Notes toward a Theory of Nostalgia: childhood and the evocation of the past in two European heritage films', *New Literary History*, Autumn, Vol. 37, Iss. 4, pp. 739 – 764.

Murray, K. And Hill, M. 1991, 'The recent history of Scottish Child Welfare, *Children and Society*, vol. 5.

Naglazas, M. 2011, 'France brought to book for nazi horror, *The West Australian*, 2 May 2011, p.7.

Natali, M.P. 2004, 'History and the Politics of Nostalgia', *Journal of Cultural Studies Iowa City*, Fall, Iss. 5, pp. 10 – 26.

National Association of Training Corps for Girls. Retrieved: 2 February 2010 from: http://en.wikipedia.org/wiki/National_Association_of_Training_Corps_for_Girls

National Statistics. Retrieved: 29 September 2007 from: http://www.statistics.gov.uk/cci/nugget.asp?id=1352.

Natt, S. 2009, 'The acceleration of Social Policies in Education and Welfare', *Children in War: the International Journal of War Children*, February, Vol. 1, No. 6.

Nikakis, G. 2005, *He's not coming home*, Griffin Press, Australia.

Nora, P. 1989, 'Between Memory and History: Les Lieux de Memoire' *Representations*, No. 26, Spring, pp.7 - 24.

Nowra, L. 2009, 'On the ever present past', *Weekend Australian Review*, January 3 – 4, p. 24.

Offer, A. 1993, 'The British empire: a waste of money?', *Economic History Review*, Vol. 46, Iss. 2, pp. 215 – 218.

O'Hagan, A. 1999, *Our Fathers*, Faber and Faber, London.

Omar, E. 2003, Truth and Reconciliation Commission, 2003, 'Truth: the road to reconciliation'. Retrieved: 19 February 2008 from http://www.doj. gov.za/trc/.

'Our evacuees: a social study by a Billeting Officer, 1940, *Aberdeen University Review*, vol. XXV11, no. 81, p. 243 and 238.

Ourglasgowstory, n.d. Retrieved: 22 February 2011 from: http://www.ourglasgowstory.com/story.php?sid=356.

Owen, A.D.K. 1944, 'The great evacuation', *The Political Quarterly*. Iss. 11, pp. 30-44.

Oxford Encyclopedia of World History, 1998, Oxford University Press, Oxford.

Palmer, G. 1997, *Reluctant Refuge*, Kangaroo Press, East Roseville.

Panter-Downes, M. 1971, *London War Notes: 1939-1945*, Farrar, Strous and Giroux.

Parliamentary Debates, 5th Series, 1939-40, vol. 362, col. 116, in Stewart, J. & Welshman, J. 2006, 'The evacuation of children in wartime Scotland: culture, behaviour and poverty', *Journal of Scottish Historical Studies*, Iss. 26, vol. 1, pp.100-120.

Parsons, M.L. 1998, *I'll take that one: dispelling the myths of civilian evacuation 1939-1945*, Beckett Karlson, Peterborough.

Parsons, M.L. 1999, *Waiting to go home*, Page Bros. Norwich.

Patinkin, D. 1984, 'Keynes and Economics Today', *American Economic Review*, vol. 74, no. 2. Retrieved: 9 March 2006 from JSTOR database.

Patton, M. 1990, *Qualitative Evaluation and Research Methods*, Sage Publications, London.

Payne, B.K. & Corrigan, E. 2007, 'Emotional constraints on intentional forgetting', *Journal of Experimental Social Psychology*, 43, pp. 780-786. Retrieved: 2 August 2009 from Science Direct database.

Perks, R. & Thomson, A. *Oral History Reader*, Routledge, London.

Perry, N. 1994, *Quotable Women*, Running Press, Philadelphia.

Pertti, K. 2004, 'The political consequences in Finland of the unexpected results of the evacuation of Finnish children to Sweden during World War Two', *Children in War*, Vol. 1, No. 4.

Pickering, M. & Keightley, E. 2006, 'The modalities of nostalgia, *Current Sociology*, Vol. 54, Iss. 6, pp. 919 – 926.

Pilcher, J. 2007, 'Body Work: childhood, gender and school health education in England, 1870 – 1977, *Childhood*, Issue 14, pp. 215 – 230.

Plumb, J.H. 1975, 'The new world of children in18th century England, *Past and Present*, no. 67, pp. 64 – 95.

Pollok, D. 2005, *Remembering: Oral History Performance*, Palgrave MacMillan, New York, USA.

Population. Retrieved: 24 October 2007 from: http://www.gro-scotland.gov.uk/files1/stats/annual-report2006/annual-report-2006pdf

Portelli, A. 1998, 'Oral history as genre', in M. Chamberlain and P. Thompson (eds) *Narrative and Genre*, Routledge, London.

Punch, K.F. 1998, *Introduction to Social Research*, Sage Publications, London.

Quinault, R. 2007, 'Scots on top?, *History Today*, July, Vol. 57, Iss. 7 pp. 30-37.

Ramirez, M.E. 2007, 'Resilience: A concept Analysis', *Nursing Forum*, vol. 42, Iss. 2, pp. 73-85.

Reading University, Research Centre for Evacuees and war child studies. Retrieved: 23 March 2006 from: http://www.extra.rdg.ac.uk/evacueesarchive/.

Registrar-General's Reviews and Annual Reports of the Health Departments 1939-1945, cited in R.Titmuss, Problems of Social Policy. Retrieved 2 June 2010 from: http://www.ibiblio.org/hyperwar/UN?UK-Civil-Social/UK-Civil-Social-7.htm.

Richardson, G.E. Neiger, B., Jensen, S., & Kumpfer, K. 1990, 'The resiliency model', *Health Education*, Iss. 21, pp. 33-39.

Richardson, G.E. 2002, 'The metatheory of resilience and resiliency, *Journal of Clinical Psychology*, Iss. 58, pp. 307 – 321.

Richards, R. 2009, 'The man who could not tell the truth, the semi-invisible man', *Biography*, Vol. 32, No. 1, pp. 190 – 290. Retrieved: 4 October 2009 from Project Muse database.

Ricoeur, P. 2004, *Memory History Forgetting*, University of Chicago Press, Chicago.

Riley, J.R. & Master, A.S. 2005, 'Resilience in context', in R. deV Peters, B.J.R. Leadbetter and R.J. McMahon, *Children, families and communities*, 32nd annual Banff International Conference on Behavioural Science held in Banff, Alberta, Canada in March 2000.

Ritchie, T.R. 1999, *Golden City: Scottish children's street games and songs'*, Mercat Press, Edinburgh.

Ritson, J. WW11, *An archive of World War Two memories – written by the public, gathered by the BBC.* Retrieved: 27 October 2007 from: http://www.bbc.co.uk/ww2peopleswar/stories/50/a5240350.shtml

Roberts, A. 2002, 'The politics and anti-politics of Nostalgia', *East European Politics and Societies.* Retrieved: 12 February 2008 from http://eep.sagepub.com

Roffey, J. 2009, Evacuation Reunion Association, email 3 February.

Roman, E. 2009, 'Post traumatic stress syndrome during World War Two 65 years on' in Parsons *Children, the Invisible victims of war,* DSM, Peterborough.

Rose, C. 2009, 'Raggedness and respectability in Barnardo's Archives', *Children in the Past: an International Journal*, vol.1, no. 1, January, pp.136-150.

Rose, L. 1991, *The Erosion of Childhood*, Routledge, London.

Rose, S. 2003 *Which people's war?* Oxford University Press, Oxford.

Ross, K. *Classic Children's Games from Scotland*, Scottish Children's Press, Dalkeith.

Ross, M. Spencer, S. Blatz C. & Restorick, E. 2008, 'Collaboration reduces the frequency of false memories in older and younger adults', *Psychology and Aging*, Vol. 23, pp. 85 – 92.

Rutter, M. 1987, 'Psychosocial resilience and protective mechanisms', *American Journal of Orthopsychiatry*, Vol. 57, (30), pp. 316 – 331.

Rutter, M. 1999, 'Resilience concepts, findings and implications for family therapy', *Journal of Family Therapy*, vol. 21, pp. 119 – 144.

Sackville-West 1994, 'The Women's Land Army' in J. Hartley, *Hearts Undefeated Women's Writing of the Second World War*, Virago Press, London.

Saffle, S. 2008, 'A happier war child story: one Finnish war child's exceptional memories and circumstances', *Children: the invisible victims of war*, DSM, Peterborough.

Salmond, A.2009, First Minister, Scottish Government, personal communication.

Samuel, R. 1994, *Theatres of memory. Volume 1. Past and present memory in contemporary culture*, Verso, London.

Sayer, A. 1994, *Method in Social Science – a realist approach*, Routledge, London.

Scarce Comics. 'History of the Beano and Dandy'. Retrieved: 10 November 2008 from http://www.scarcecomics.com/auction/beanodandyhist.asp.

Schacter, D. 1995, *Searching for memory, the brain, the mind, and the past*, Basic, New York.

Schoenhals, M. 2005, 'Why don't we arm the Left? Mao's culpability for the Cultural Revolution's "Great Chaos" of 1967', *The China Quarterly*, June, Iss. 182, p. 277.

Schofield, G. & Beek, M. 2005, 'Risk and resilience in long-term foster care', *British Journal of Social Work*, Iss. 35, pp. 1283 – 1301. Retrieved: 25 March 2008 from Proquest database.

Schouten, F. 2006, 'Individual and collective memory in *Escenas de cine mudo* by Julio Llamzares, *Neophilologus*, 90, pp. 271 – 281.

Scot.gov, 'Housing return for Scotland (various years)'. Retrieved: 30 July 2008 from: Titmuss, R.M. 1950, *The Problems of Social Policy*. Retrieved: 28 June 2005 from: http://www.scotland.gov.uk/library/documents-w7/hgp-04.htm http://www.ibiblio.org/hyperwar/UN?UK-Civil-Social/UK-Civil-Social-7.htm.

Scotland Office.gov.uk Retrieved: 10 March 2006 from: http://www.scotland-office.gov.uk/history/scotland-office.html.

Scotland.gov.uk. Retrieved: 16 June 2009 from: http://www.Scotland.gov.uk/News/News-Extras/inholyrood

Scottish National Party, 'It's time'. Retrieved: 19 May 2007 from:http://www.snp.org/.

Scottish Parliament.gov.uk. Retrieved: 25 October 2007 from: http://www. scottish.parliament.uk/business/research/factsheets/documents/MSPsA-Session1.pdf.

Seabrook, J. 1982, *Working class childhood*, Victor Bollancz Ltd, London.

Sennett, R. 1998, 'Disturbing Memories' in P. Fara and K. Patterson, *Memory*, Cambridge University Press, Melbourne.

Sharp, P. 2008, 'How the children lost their milk' in P. Starns 2008, *Children: the invisible victims of war*, DSM, Peterborough.

Shields, C. 2008, *The Stone diaries*, Fourth Estate, London.

Silverman, D. 1993, *Interpreting Qualitative Data, Methods for Analysing Talk, Text and Interaction*, Sage Publications, London.

Simmons, M. 2006, 'British WW11 Child Evacuees – revisited, revisioned and repositioned' *The International Journal for Child and War Studies*, vol 1, no. 4, pp. 51 – 59.

Simmons, M. 2008, 'Paying the Piper: Female British WW11 Evacuees tell their mother's stories', *Children: the invisible victims of war*, The Studio, Peterborough.

Singer, N. 2007, 'The U.S.S.R. is coming back (at least on clothing racks)', *New York Times*, 27 November, p. A1.

Smith, D. 2007, 'Official responses to juvenile delinquency in Scotland during Second World War', *Twentieth Century British History*, vol. 18, no. 1, pp.78-105.

Spiegel, G.N. 2007, 'Revising the past/revisiting the present: how change happens in Historiography', *History and Theory*, Theme Iss. 46, pp. 1 – 19.

Speier, M. 1992, 'The everyday world of the child', in C. Jenks, *The sociology of childhood*, Gregg Revivals, Hampshire.

Starkey, P. 2000, 'The Feckless Mother: women, poverty and social workers in wartime and post-war England', *Women's History Review*, vol. 9. No. 3, pp. 539 - 555.

Starns, P. 2008, 'Boots for the bairns', in M. Parsons, *Children: the invisible victims of war*, The Studio, Peterborough.

Statistics.gov.uk, 2005, Retrieved: 8 August 2005 from: http://www.statistics.gov.uk/census2001/downloads/pop2001ew.pdf.

Stewart, P. 2005, *Images of Scotland*, Tempus Publishing, Stroud.

Stewart, J. 2001, 'The most precious possession of a nation is its children': the Clyde Committee on Homeless Children in Scotland', *Scottish Economic and Social History*, Vol.21, Iss.1.

Tannock, S. 1995, 'Nostalgia Critique', *Cultural Studies*, vol. 9, Iss. 3, October, pp. 453 – 464.

Taylor, A.J.P. 1972, *The origins of the Second World War*, Hamish Hamilton, London.

Tebbutt, M. 1997, *Women's Talk? A social history of 'Gossip' in working class neighbourhoods, 1880-1960*, Manchester Metropolitan University, U.K.

The British Parliament, 2006. Retrieved: 20 February 2006 from http://www.parliament.uk/.

The complete illustrated poems, songs and Ballads of Robert Burns, 1990. Chancellor Press, London.

The Macquarie Dictionary, 1997, 3rd edition, the Macquarie Library, New South Wales.

The Perthshire Advertiser, 1939 20 September (cited in S. Robertson and L. Wilson, 1995, *Scotland's War*, p.16).

The Scottish Government, 'Education and Training in Scotland National Dossier 2005. Retrieved: 20 January 2011 from: http://www.scotland.gov.uk/Publications/2005/06/13113114/31273

The Wartime Memories Project. Retrieved: 7 July 2008 from: http://www. wartimememories.co.uk/.

Thompson, P. 1998, 'Oral history as genre', in M. Chamberlain and P. Thompson (eds) *Narrative and Genre*, Routledge, London.

Tilly, C. 1975, *The formation of national states in Western Europe*, Princeton University Press, New Jersey.

Titmuss, R.M. 1950, *The Problems of Social Policy*. Retrieved: 28 June 2005 from: http://www.ibiblio.org/hyperwar/UN?UK-Civil-Social/UK-Civil-Social-7.htm.

Traqair, P. 2000. *Freedom's Sword*, HarperCollins, London.

Trevor-Roper, H. 2008, *The invention of Scotland*, Yale University Press, New Haven.

Turnbull, A. 2000, 'Collaboration and censorship in the oral history interview', *International Journal of Social Research Methodology*, vol. 3, no. 1, pp. 15-34. Retrieved: 12 January 2007 from Taylor & Francis database.

UK National Statistics Hub. Retrieved: 18 January 2007 from: http://www.statistics.gov.uk/hub/index.html.

Union History Timeline, 'From illegality to a role in government: a trade union timeline'. Retrieved: 21 February 2011 from http://www.unionancestors.co.uk/Timeline.htm

United Nations.org. Retrieved: 27 February 2008 from http://www.un.org /rights/dpil765e.htm.

United Nations.org. Retrieved: 10 January 2011 from: http://www.un.org/ works/goingon/soldiers/childsoldiersmap.html

University of Essex, Hist.pop. Retrieved: 7 August 2009 from http:hist pop.org./ohpr.servlet/PageBrowser?path=Browse/Census.

Vessey, B. 2003, 'Disarmament, security and rearmament. 1919-38:could you disarm and still ensure international security? This was what British ministers between the wars desperately need to find out', *Modern History Review*, 'April, vol. 14, iss. 4, pp. 26-30. Retrieved: 26 Feb 2006 from Infotrac database.

Wartime Memories Project.gov.uk. Retrieved: 4 August 2009 from: http://www.wartimememories.co.uk/ships/cityofbenares.html.

Weber, M. 1978, *Economy and society: an outline of interpretive sociology*, University of California Press, Berkeley.

Welshman, J. 1999, 'Evacuation hygiene and social policy: the *Our Town* Report of 1943', *Historical Journal*, vol. 43, No. 3, pp. 781 – 807.

Westall, R. 1995, *Children of the Blitz*, MacMillan Children's Books, Middlesex.

White, E. 2008, 'The evacuation of children from Leningrad during World War Two', *Children, the invisible victims of war*, DMC, Peterborough.

Wicks, B. 1988, *No time to wave goodbye*, St Martin's Press, New York.

Winkler, K. 1995, 'Conducting the "sensitive" interview', *The Writer*, Jan., vol. 108, no. 1, pp. 18-21.

Winter, J. 2006, *Remembering War, the Great War between Memory and History in the Twentieth Century*, Yale University Press, New Haven.

Wolf, D. 2007, *Beyond Anne Frank*, University of California Press, Berkeley, Los Angeles.

Women in Quote, Anthology, 1993, Axiom Publishing, South Australia.

Women's Voluntary Service. Retrieved: 4 July 2006 from: http://amynelson. co.uk/womenswiki/index.php?title=Women's_voluntary_service.

'World War 2 Commemoration in Gdansk', *The Sophia Echo*. Retrieved: 9 November 2009 from: http://sofiaecho.com/2009/09/01/777327_world-war-2-commemoration-in-gdansk

Young, J. 1993, *Texture of Memory, Holocaust memory and meaning*, Yale University Press, New Haven.

Zelizer, B. 1995, 'Reading the past against the grain', *Critical Studies in Mass Communication*, Iss. 12, pp. 214 – 319.